Unleashing India's Potential

70 HR Weekly Workhour

DIBYENDU CHOUDHURY

Disclaimer

This book is intended to provide general information and guidance on how to do business in India. It is not a substitute for professional advice or services. The author and the publisher do not guarantee the accuracy, completeness, or suitability of the information and opinions expressed in this book for any specific purpose or situation. The reader is advised to consult with a qualified professional before taking any action based on the contents of this book.

The author and the publisher are not responsible for any errors or omissions in this book or for any consequences arising from the use of this book. The author and the publisher do not endorse or recommend any products, services, websites, or organizations mentioned in this book. The views and opinions expressed in this book are solely those of the author and do not necessarily reflect those of the publisher or any other person or entity.

The author and the publisher have taken all reasonable care to ensure that the information and opinions in this book are current and accurate as of the date of publication. However, the business environment in India is constantly changing and evolving. Therefore, the reader is advised to verify the latest developments and updates before relying on any information or opinion in this book.

This book is protected by copyright laws. No part of this book may be reproduced, distributed, transmitted, or stored in any form or by any means without the prior written permission of the author and the publisher.

You can use the information in this book for academic purposes if you acknowledge the source and give proper credit to the author and the publisher. You should also follow academic writing and citation's ethical and legal norms. You should not copy, plagiarize, or misrepresent any information or opinion in this book. You should also respect the author's and the publisher's intellectual property rights.

Tribute and Dedication

The recent discussions ignited by prominent figures like Padma Shri and Padma Bhushan Shri Narayana Murthy and Padma Shri Mrs. Sudha Murty have sparked a fiery debate on the significance of hard work, the correlation between working hours and productivity, and the vital role of patriotism in shaping a nation's destiny. Their thought-provoking insights have not only stirred conversations but have also inspired deeper reflections on how these elements contribute to both personal and national growth.

Shri Narayana Murthy's comments on the "70-hour work week" have particularly highlighted the complex dynamics between working hours and productivity. This has led to widespread discussions on whether longer workdays genuinely enhance output or lead to burnout and reduced efficiency. These debates underscore the importance of finding a balance that promotes both high performance and well-being among workers.

Furthermore, the discussions have brought to light the integral role of patriotism and dedication to one's country in driving progress and development. The values and principles championed by Shri Narayana Murthy and Mrs. Sudha Murty emphasize the significance of commitment, perseverance, and a sense of duty towards the nation.

Considering these impactful conversations and the

fundamental questions raised by Shri Narayana Murthy's comments, this book is dedicated to showing my respect and tribute to him and his family members. Their unwavering dedication to hard work, their pioneering contributions to the industry, and their profound influence on societal values have been a source of inspiration for many.

This dedication also recognizes the Murthy family's broader contributions to education, social work, and nation-building. Mrs. Sudha Murty's extensive philanthropic efforts and literary contributions further exemplify the values of compassion, empathy, and service to society. Their combined efforts have created a legacy that continues to inspire and guide individuals and communities alike.

Through this book, I aim to explore the essential questions raised by Shri Narayana Murthy and to delve into the broader implications of his comments. It is my sincere hope that this work not only honors their contributions but also adds to the ongoing dialogue about the relationship between work, productivity, and national progress.

In dedicating this book to the Murthy family, I express my deep admiration and gratitude for their tireless efforts and exemplary leadership. Their vision and commitment serve as a beacon of inspiration, encouraging us all to strive for excellence, uphold strong ethical standards, and contribute positively to society and our nation.

Contents

CONTENTS

CONTENTS

Foreword from the Author

In the intricate tapestry that weaves together the threads of work ethic, productivity and national development, we often find ourselves at crossroads, navigating the delicate balance between dedication and burnout, striving for success while mindful of the importance of a harmonious work-life equilibrium. The recent discussions[1] ignited by prominent figures like Padmashree & Padma Bibhushan Shri Narayana Murthy and Padmashree Mrs. Sudha Murty have sparked a fiery debate on the significance of hard work, the correlation between working hours and productivity and the vital role of patriotism in shaping a nation's destiny.

As we immerse ourselves in the diverse perspectives presented within these pages, we are invited to delve into the heart of these intricate narratives, exploring the profound impact of labour productivity, Gross Manufacturing Value Added (GMVA) and the multifaceted dimensions of patriotism on a nation's economic growth and societal fabric. Through meticulous analysis and insightful reflections, this book endeavors to unravel the complexities surrounding these pivotal themes, shedding light on the interconnected dynamics that drive progress and development in our ever-evolving world.

---

[1] *https://www.ndtv.com/india-news/narayana-murthy-says-western-friends-nris-agree-with-48hour-work-advice-4803447*

From the call for longer working hours as a catalyst for national productivity to the imperative to strike a delicate balance between dedication to work and holistic well-being, each chapter unravels a narrative thread that resonates with the aspirations and challenges of individuals and nations striving for excellence amidst a backdrop of shifting paradigms and emerging opportunities.

Through the kaleidoscope of perspectives presented within these chapters, we are beckoned to reexamine our preconceptions, challenge our assumptions and embark on a journey of introspection and discovery. As we navigate the contours of labour productivity, GMVA enhancement strategies and the significance of fostering a deep-rooted sense of patriotism, we are reminded of the transformative power that lies in unity, resilience and unwavering commitment to a shared vision of progress and prosperity.

As we embark on this intellectual odyssey, may we heed the call to embrace the nuances of change, the wisdom of experience and the vibrancy of innovation. Let us embark on this exploration with open minds, curious spirits and a shared dedication to unravelling the mysteries that lie at the intersection of dedication, productivity and national pride.

In the pages that follow, let us embark on a journey of enlightenment, dialogue and discovery—an odyssey that promises to illuminate the path towards a future where hard work, productivity and patriotism converge to shape a world brimming with promise, potential and endless possibilities.

Are you ready?

Let us begin.

Dr. Dibyendu Choudhury

P.S: For any comments or clarifications the author can be reached anytime through his website www.dibyenduchoudhury.com

BUSINESS & ECONOMICS

70 HR WEEKLY WORKHOUR

INTRODUCTION

Sab ka Saath Saab ka Vikash 3.0

Chapter 1: Introduction

Infosys founder Padmashree and Padma Bibhushan Shri Narayana Murthy recently ignited a social media furore with his advice to young people to work "70 hours a week." Sudha Murty, chairperson of the Infosys Foundation and novelist, has joined the ongoing social media spat. Murthy's counsel urged young people to work "70 hours a week." Sudha Murty stated that the founder of Infosys has worked 80–90 hours per week in the past and that he is a firm believer in putting in genuine effort. She also emphasized the importance of hard work and dedication in achieving success, echoing her husband's sentiments. Sudha Murty further added that while working long hours is important, it is equally crucial to maintain a healthy work-life balance. She encouraged young people to find a job they are passionate about, as it will make putting in those long hours much more fulfilling. Overall, both Narayana and Sudha Murty's advice serves as a reminder that success does not come easy and requires dedication and perseverance.

Because he has consistently worked between 80 and 90 hours each week, he is unable to comprehend the concept of working fewer hours. He is an advocate of genuine toil and he led his life accordingly. "As a result, he has expressed his true feelings," Murty told News18. When asked if she tried to explain how things work in corporate India these days, she said that people have different methods of expressing themselves, but Narayana Murthy has worked long hours and offered his expertise.

 Murty also mentioned that, despite the changing work culture in corporate India, Narayana Murthy remains steadfast in his belief that hard work is the key to success. She acknowledged that, while some may view his dedication as extreme, she admires his commitment to his work and principles. She concluded by stating that Narayana Murthy's work ethic serves as an inspiration to many aspiring entrepreneurs and professionals.

Narayana Murthy's comments about the productivity of young people in India sparked a heated online discussion after they were posted on social media. Murthy had mentioned in a recent podcast that young people will need to put in a full twelve hours of labour each and every day in order for India to be able to compete with countries that have made remarkable strides in the past two to three decades. He went on to assert[2] that India has one of the lowest productivity rates in the world. Therefore, as a result of this, my request is that our younger generation should declare, this is my nation." Murthy has previously stated on the podcast, "I'd like to work 70 hours per week."

---

[2] *https://indianexpress.com/article/opinion/columns/narayana-murthy-and-70-hour-work-week-a-narrow-idea-of-nation-building-9009300/*

"I'd like to work 70 hours a week." To be able to compete with countries such as China[3], he added, younger generations need to increase the number of hours they spend working, just as Japan and Germany did after World War II. This transformation[4] has to come to youngsters because youngsters are a significant majority of our population at this point in time and they are the ones who can build our country, he added in conclusion. Murthy went on to say that India's working population needs to transition into people who are highly determined, extremely disciplined and extremely hard-working.

This debate inspired the concept for my bookend I am still keen to learn more about the relationship between working hours and productivity, which has always been a complex one that has raised multiple eyebrows, sparked debates in the past and will continue to do so. Murthy, a successful entrepreneur, feels that teaching these values to the youth will eventually assist the country's economic and general development.

I expect that by investigating the relationship between working hours and productivity, we might find useful insights for both individuals and businesses seeking to increase efficiency and

---

[3] https://www.cnn.com/india-infosys-founder-work-hours-success-intl-hnk/index.html

[4] https://www.livemint.com/economy/from-60-hours-in-2020-narayana-murthy-now-suggests-70-hour-work-week-for-youngsters-where-will-he-go-next-11698339720990.html

success. Despite the potential issues and discussions surrounding this topic, let us delve into it further to find the insights that remain for the future of work in India.

Working longer hours

While working longer hours can lead to increased output, it can also lead to burnout, fatigue and decreased productivity. In fact, data from developed, industrialized nations shows that they have a higher level of productivity with fewer hours worked, while emerging markets see a lower level of employee productivity[5] and an increased number of hours worked. Now there is always scoped to question those international organizations that give such rankings and release such dates from time to time so that they can prove their supremacy. It has been constantly proven wrong several times that those data releases are highly motivated and incentivized to grab the market or sell their products or services in India. It is important to consider the motives behind the data released by international organizations and to question the validity of their rankings. In the case of productivity statistics, it is clear that there are discrepancies between developed and emerging markets that cannot be ignored. Instead of blindly accepting these rankings, it is crucial to analyze the factors at play and consider the larger implications for global economies. Ultimately, a more nuanced understanding of

---

[5] *https://humanyze.com/blog-employee-productivity-vs-hours-worked-whats-the-difference/*

productivity and work culture is necessary to accurately assess the true state of affairs in different regions. For example, when looking at productivity rankings that place a developed country at the top, it is important to question whether factors such as automation and technology are artificially inflating their numbers. Conversely, in emerging markets where manual labour may still be prevalent, traditional productivity metrics may not accurately reflect the overall efficiency of their workforce.

It's important to note that productivity is measured as GDP per hour of work. Therefore, it's not just the number of hours worked those matters, but also the quality of work and the efficiency of the workforce. Labor productivity is measured as GDP per hour of work[6]. GDP is adjusted for inflation and differences in cost of living between countries. Data comparing specific countries reveals that many developed, industrialized nations have better levels of productivity with less hours worked, whereas emerging markets have lower levels of employee productivity and more hours spent. This emphasizes the significance of investing in education and training programs to develop labour skills and knowledge, which will ultimately lead to increased

---

[6] *https://ourworldindata.org/grapher/labor-productivity-per-hour-pennworldtable Labor productivity measures the amount of*

production. Furthermore, using technology and automation can improve efficiency and productivity. By concentrating on these variables, governments can work to increase overall productivity and remain competitive in the global marketplace. Policymakers and businesses must emphasize productivity growth to drive economic progress and prosperity.

Both labour productivity and gross merchandise volume (GMV) are important for a nation's economy, but they measure different things. Labor productivity measures[7] the amount of goods and services produced per hour of work, while GMV measures the total value of goods sold[8] by a company or an industry. Both metrics are essential for understanding and improving the overall performance of an economy. By increasing labour productivity, a country can produce more with the same amount of resources, leading to higher economic output and growth. On the other hand, a higher GMV indicates increased sales and revenue, which can boost economic activity and create more opportunities for businesses and workers. By monitoring and enhancing both labour productivity and GMV, countries can work towards achieving sustainable economic development and prosperity in the long run. For example, a manufacturing company implementing automation technology to

---

[7] *https://quickonomics.com/terms/output-per-hour-worked/*
[8] *https://fastercapital.com/topics/understanding-gross-merchandise-value-(gmv).html*

increase labour productivity could see a significant rise in their GMV as they are able to produce more goods at a faster rate. This, in turn, can lead to increased profits, job creation and overall economic growth within the industry and the country as a whole.

Higher labour productivity means that a country is producing more goods and services per hour of work, which can lead to higher economic growth and higher wages for workers. On the other hand, higher GMV means that a company or an industry is selling more goods, which can lead to higher profits and more investment in the business. Ultimately, the combination of higher labour productivity and GMV can create a positive feedback loop for businesses and the economy. As companies become more efficient and produce more goods, they are able to generate higher revenues and profits. This allows them to reinvest in their operations, expand their workforce and contribute to overall economic growth. Additionally, higher wages for workers can lead to increased consumer spending, further driving demand for goods and services. Overall, these factors work together to create a more prosperous and dynamic economy.

Therefore, both labour productivity and GMV are important for a nation's economy, but they measure different aspects of economic activity.

> ➢ Labor productivity is measured as GDP per hour of work. GDP is adjusted for inflation

and for differences in the cost of living between countries.

- ➢ Higher labour productivity can lead to higher economic growth and higher wages for workers.
- ➢ GMV measures the total value of goods sold by a company or an industry.

Gross Manufacturing Value Added (GMVA) is an important indicator of a country's economic growth. It measures the value added by the manufacturing sector to the gross domestic product (GDP) of a country. According to the data from the U.S. Bureau of Economic Analysis, the manufacturing sector contributed 10.9% of the GDP in the first quarter of 2023. A higher GMVA indicates a strong manufacturing sector, which can lead to job creation, increased exports and overall economic expansion. This, in turn, can have a positive impact on the standard of living for workers and contribute to a more robust economy. Therefore, policymakers and government officials often closely monitor GMVA as a key metric for assessing the health and growth potential of a country's economy. By focusing on strategies to increase GMVA, such as investing in technology, infrastructure and workforce development, countries can work towards achieving sustainable economic growth and prosperity for their citizens.

However, it is important to note that a high GMVA does not always guarantee economic prosperity for all citizens. For example, a country with a high

GMVA due to the exploitation of natural resources (Alvarado, R., Toledo, E.; 2017)[9] may experience environmental degradation and the displacement of indigenous communities, leading to social unrest and inequality. Thus, simply focusing on increasing GMVA without considering the broader social and environmental impacts can result in unsustainable growth and long-term negative consequences for the economy. This illustration could also go so far as to illustrate how a nation or business should disregard the social advancement and development of other developing nations by using them as a product disposal site. This lack of consideration for the well-being of marginalized communities not only perpetuates inequality but also hinders overall global progress. It is essential for nations and businesses to prioritize sustainable development that considers social, environmental and economic factors in order to ensure long-term prosperity for all stakeholders involved. By shifting towards a more inclusive and responsible approach to growth, we can create a more equitable and sustainable future for generations to come.

While GMVA is an important indicator of economic growth, it is not the only one. Other indicators, such as labour productivity, employment rate and inflation rate, are also important for measuring the overall health of an economy.

---

[9] Alvarado, R., Toledo, E. Environmental degradation and economic growth: evidence for a developing country. Environ Dev Sustain **19**, 1205–1218 (2017). https://doi.org/10.1007/s10668-016-9790-y

Therefore, it's important to consider multiple indicators when evaluating the economic performance of a country. This holistic approach to measuring economic growth allows policymakers to make informed decisions that benefit all aspects of society. By considering a variety of indicators, we can better understand the complexities of an economy and work towards creating policies that promote sustainable development. Ultimately, the goal is to achieve balanced growth that benefits both current and future generations while also safeguarding the environment and promoting social equity.

Gross Manufacturing Value Added (GMVA) measures the value added by the manufacturing sector to the gross domestic product (GDP) of a country. The manufacturing sector contributed 10.9% of the GDP in the first quarter of 2023. Other indicators, such as labour productivity, employment rate and inflation rate, are also important for measuring the overall health of an economy. For a country to achieve sustainable development, it is crucial to not only focus on economic growth but also consider social and environmental factors. By monitoring indicators like GMVA, labour productivity, employment rate and inflation rate, policymakers can make informed decisions to ensure that growth is inclusive and environmentally sustainable. It is important to strike a balance between economic development and social well-being to create a future that is prosperous for all.

Therefore, Mr. Murthy's statement had three components to further delve into this topic.

a) Longer Working Hours

b) National Productivity

and

c) India to compete in the Global Market

So, my sincere efforts will be trying to evaluate the couple of vital questions through this book.

Gross Manufacturing Value Added (GMVA)

Improving Gross Manufacturing Value Added (GMVA) for a nation can be a complex process that involves various factors. Here are some ways that can help improve GMVA:

1. Investing in technology: Investing in new technologies can help increase the efficiency of the manufacturing process, reduce costs and improve the quality of products.

2. Improving infrastructure: Improving infrastructure such as roads, ports and airports can help reduce transportation costs and improve the supply chain, which can lead to increased productivity and competitiveness.

3. Providing training and education: Providing training and education to the workforce can help improve their skills and knowledge, which can lead to increased productivity and innovation.

4. Encouraging innovation: Encouraging innovation through research and development can help create new products and processes, which can lead to increased competitiveness and growth.

5. Promoting exports: Promoting exports can help increase demand for domestically produced goods, which can lead to increased production and economic growth.

These are just some of the ways that can help improve GMVA for a nation. However, it's important to note that the effectiveness of these strategies can vary depending on the specific circumstances of each country.

The government of India has taken purposeful initiatives in the above-mentioned direction to create a nation. They have implemented policies to encourage innovation, attract foreign investment and promote exports through trade agreements and partnerships. These efforts have already started to show results, with India's GDP growth rate steadily increasing over the past few years. By focusing on improving GMVA, India is positioning itself as a strong player in the global economy and paving the way for sustainable economic development in the future.

1. Make in India initiative: This initiative aims to promote domestic manufacturing and attract foreign investment in the country.

2. Industrial Corridor Development Programme: This programme aims to develop industrial corridors across the country to promote manufacturing and create employment opportunities.

3. Ease of Doing Business: The government has implemented several reforms to improve the ease of doing business in the country, which can help attract more investment and promote growth.

4. National Single Window System: This system aims to simplify the process of obtaining clearances and approvals for setting up a business in the country.

5. PM Gati Shakti National Master Plan (NMP): This plan aims to develop a multi-modal transportation system to improve connectivity and reduce logistics costs.

6. National Logistics Policy: This policy aims to create a single-window e-logistics market and improve the efficiency of the logistics sector.

7. Indian Footwear and Leather Development Programme (IFLDP): This programme aims to promote the development of the footwear and leather industry in the country.

8. Raising and amplifying the MSME Performance (RAMP) initiative is also a key focus for the government, aiming to support and enhance the performance of micro, small and medium enterprises (MSMEs) in India. These initiatives collectively work towards creating a conducive environment for businesses to thrive and contribute to the overall economic growth of the country. By streamlining processes, reducing costs and providing necessary support, the government is actively working towards making India a more attractive destination for investments and entrepreneurship.

These initiatives can help improve the Gross Manufacturing Value Added (GMVA) of the country by promoting domestic manufacturing, attracting foreign investment and improving the ease of doing business. However, it's important to note that the effectiveness of these initiatives can vary depending on the specific circumstances of each industry and region.

Patriotism is another important emotion that has been around since the dawn of time and it is still relevant today. It can be defined as a feeling of love, loyalty and devotion to one's country. Patriotism is essential for any nation in order to ensure its stability, security and development. It fosters a sense of community and shared values among citizens and encourages them to work together for the betterment of their country. It also inspires individuals to take pride in their country's achievements and contribute to its continued success.

However, it's important to note that patriotism should not be confused with nationalism. While patriotism emphasizes unity and constructive pride, nationalism often fuels division and an ethnocentric attitude. Therefore, it's important to nurture a sense of patriotism anchored in shared values such as respect for human rights, democracy and the rule of law. This kind of patriotism promotes inclusivity and diversity, recognizing that a country's strength lies in the variety of its people and perspectives. By upholding these core values, individuals can come together to address challenges and celebrate successes as a united front. In essence, patriotism should serve as a unifying force that transcends individual differences and fosters a sense of belonging and responsibility towards the greater good of society. Ultimately, a healthy sense of patriotism can lead to a more cohesive and harmonious community, where everyone feels valued and empowered to contribute positively towards a common goal.

In conclusion, patriotism is an important factor for a nation's growth and development. It fosters a sense of unity, shared identity and responsibility among citizens, which can lead to increased productivity, innovation and social harmony.

As a result, this book will explore a few questions, as listed below and we will attempt to go into these themes.

1. Is it the working hours or the productivity of the nation?

2. Is labour productivity, or GMV, important for the nation?

3. Gross Manufacturing Value-added growth is more important than anything else.

4. How can we improve GMVA for a nation?

5. The government of India is also thinking in the same direction and has taken several schemes to improve GMVA.?

6. Enhancing patriotism is another factor that we cannot overlook; unless we love our own country, nothing is possible?

7. Which factors are important in improving patriotism?

8. Can a nation think about patriotism when the majority of the people live below the poverty line?

Factors such as education, culture, history and national pride all play a role in improving patriotism. However, it is difficult for a nation to prioritize patriotism when a large portion of its population is struggling to meet basic needs due to poverty. It is important for the government to address poverty and provide opportunities for economic growth in order to create a sense of unity and pride among its citizens. Only then can patriotism truly flourish and contribute to the overall improvement of the nation.

70 HR WEEKLY WORKHOUR

ROLE OF WORKING HOURS & PRODUCTIVITY

Chapter-2

Chapter 2: The Role of Working Hours

 In the context of developing nations, the interplay between working hours and productivity is a critical consideration. Both factors significantly impact economic growth, individual well-being and overall societal progress.

Excessive working hours can lead to burnout, decreased productivity and a negative impact on mental and physical health. On the other hand, insufficient working hours can result in low wages, poverty and limited opportunities for economic advancement. Finding the right balance in working hours is essential for promoting sustainable development and ensuring the well-being of workers in developing nations.

In addition to the quantity of working hours, the quality of those hours is also crucial. Factors such as job flexibility, job security and work-life balance play a significant role in determining the overall well-being of workers. A work environment that values employee health and happiness can lead to increased job satisfaction, higher productivity and reduced turnover rates. Furthermore, investing in employee training and development can help workers acquire new skills and advance their careers, ultimately contributing to economic growth and social progress. By prioritizing both the quantity and quality of working hours, policymakers and businesses can create a more sustainable and equitable workforce that benefits both individuals and society as a whole.

Quantity vs. Quality:

- Working hours refer to the time individuals spend engaged in labour. Historically, longer working hours were often associated with higher productivity. However, this relationship is more nuanced.

- Japan, known for its long working hours, provides an interesting case study. Research has shown that when workers already have extended workweeks, adding more hours can actually reduce productivity.

- During World War I in Britain, women working on piece rates in artillery shell manufacturing demonstrated a similar pattern. While additional hours initially increased production, there was a point beyond which productivity declined due to worker fatigue and exhaustion.

Thus, the relationship between productivity and working hours follows an inverted U shape, where there is an optimal level of work hours that maximizes productivity. This highlights the importance of balancing work hours to ensure both efficiency and employee well-being. Companies that prioritize work-life balance are more likely to see higher levels of productivity and employee satisfaction in the long run. In conclusion, understanding the complexities of the relationship between working hours and productivity is crucial for achieving success in the workplace.

The Modern Workplace:

- In today's complex work environments, the relationship between hours and productivity extends beyond individual tasks.

- Team-oriented settings play a crucial role. A recent study in a Japanese architectural design firm revealed that shorter working hours led to increased team productivity.

- Interestingly, as demand declined during the Global Crisis of 2008-2009, the firm concentrated working hours within teams. Fewer team members worked shorter hours, resulting in improved productivity.

- Less is more: Reducing working hours can enhance individual productivity and reduce mistakes at work. Moreover, clocking in fewer hours can also boost employee morale and job satisfaction, leading to a more positive work environment.

This shift towards prioritizing quality over quantity has been shown to not only improve overall productivity but also increase employee retention rates. Ultimately, finding the right balance between working hours and productivity is essential for the success of both individuals and teams in complex work environments.

The Significance of Productivity

1. Beyond Clocking Hours:

- Productivity transcends mere time spent working. It is an attribute of skill, knowledge and efficiency.

- Human capital, including education, training, health and nutrition, enhances labour's ability to generate greater value within the same time frame.

- Technological advancements also contribute significantly to productivity gains. When individuals are able to work smarter, not just harder, they can accomplish more in less time, leading to increased productivity.

- Teams that prioritize efficiency and effectiveness in their work processes are able to achieve their goals more quickly and with higher quality results.

- Ultimately, the significance of productivity lies in its ability to drive success and growth in both personal and professional endeavors.

By focusing on maximizing productivity, individuals and teams can not only achieve their objectives more efficiently, but also create more opportunities for innovation and growth. Productivity is not just about getting more work done in less time, but also about improving the quality and impact of the work being produced. When productivity is prioritized, it becomes a key driver of success and a catalyst for progress in all aspects of life.

2. Labor Productivity and Economic Growth:

- GDP per hour of work measures labour productivity. Adjusted for inflation and cost of living, it reflects the value created by each hour of labour.

- Developing nations must focus on enhancing human capital to boost productivity.

- Policies that promote education, skill development and innovation are crucial for sustainable economic growth. By investing in education and skill development, countries can improve their workforce's productivity and ultimately drive economic growth. Innovation is also key in increasing productivity, as new technologies and processes can streamline work and increase efficiency. Overall, prioritizing labour productivity is essential for fostering economic development and creating a thriving society.

Balancing working hours and productivity is essential for any developing nation. While longer hours may seem productive initially, diminishing returns set in due to fatigue. Prioritizing quality over quantity, investing in human CapitaLand fostering innovation will drive sustainable progress. Ultimately, it is the synergy between efficient working hours and enhanced productivity that propels nations toward prosperity. By investing in training and skill development, workers can become more efficient and effective in their roles, leading to higher productivity levels. Additionally, encouraging a healthy work-life balance can prevent burnout and improve overall well-being, ultimately leading to increased productivity in the long run. By focusing on these factors, developing nations can create a strong foundation for economic growth and success.

In the context of developing nations, the interplay between working hours and productivity is a critical consideration. Both factors significantly impact economic growth, individual well-being and overall societal progress. Let us delve into this multifaceted topic. One key aspect to consider is the importance of implementing policies that promote fair working hours and flexibility in the workplace. By allowing employees to have a better balance between their professional and personal lives, they are more likely to feel motivated and engaged in their work. This can lead to higher job satisfaction and ultimately, increased productivity. Furthermore, investing in resources and support for mental health and wellness can also play a crucial role in improving productivity levels and overall economic success in developing nations. By addressing these factors, countries can create a positive and sustainable environment for growth and advancement.

One key aspect of promoting work-life balance is offering remote work options or flexible scheduling. This allows employees to better manage their time and responsibilities, leading to decreased stress and burnout. Additionally, providing access to mental health resources, such as counseling services or wellness programs, can help employees cope with the pressures of work and improve their overall well-being. When employees feel supported and valued in both their professional and personal lives, they are more likely to be productive and contribute positively to the success of their organization. Ultimately, prioritizing employee well-being can have a ripple effect on the economy as a whole, leading to increased innovation, creativity and success.

1. Long Working Hours:

- The   International Labour Organization (ILO) reports that the proportion of workers with excessively long hours is   twice as high   in developing countries compared to developed ones.

-    Low wages drive this phenomenon. Workers often need to work extended hours to make ends meet.

2. Quality of Work:

- While reducing unemployment globally, improvements in the quality of work lag behind. Poor working conditions persist, affecting productivity and well-being.

- Ensuring decent working conditions is crucial for sustainable development.

3. Balancing Productivity and Fatigue:

- Developing nations face the challenge of balancing productivity with worker fatigue.

- Longer hours may seem productive initially, but beyond a point, diminishing returns occur due to exhaustion.

4. Human Capital Investment:

- Enhancing human capital is essential for productivity growth.

- Policies promoting education, skill development and health contribute to sustainable economic progress.

5. Global Coordination:

- Multinational companies operating across time zones struggle to find common working hours.

- Utilizing tools like shared calendars and time zone converters helps coordinate meetings effectively.

6. Recovery Stagnation:

- As countries relaxed COVID-19 measures, hours worked increased but remained below pre-pandemic levels.

- New variants and lockdown reintroductions hindered full recovery.

7. Legal Frameworks:

- Developing nations must establish robust labour laws to protect workers' rights.

- Balancing flexibility with worker well-being is crucial.

This includes setting limits on working hours, ensuring fair wages and providing safe working conditions. Additionally, enforcing these laws and holding employers accountable is essential in creating a healthy and sustainable work environment. By prioritizing both productivity and employee well-being, countries can strive towards a more balanced and equitable workforce.

Technology Implementation helps Productivity

Technology plays a crucial role in managing work hours by enhancing efficiency, streamlining processes and promoting productivity. Here are some ways technology available:

1. Task Management Tools:

- Apps and software help organize and prioritize tasks. Tools like Trello or Asana allows teams to collaborate effectively and track progress.

2. Time Tracking:

- Time management apps assist in monitoring work hours. They help individuals allocate time efficiently and stay on track.

3. Automation:

- Technology automates repetitive tasks, freeing up time for more valuable work.

- Automated reminders ensure deadlines are met and meetings are attended.

4. Remote Work:

- Communication tools like Slack, Microsoft Teams and Zoom enable seamless collaboration across geographies.

- Virtual workspaces facilitate remote work, allowing employees to manage their hours flexibly.

5. Data-Driven Insights:

- Technology provides analytics on work patterns, identifying areas for improvement.

- Insights help optimize work schedules and allocate resources effectively.

6. Performance Management:

- Performance tracking software evaluates employee productivity.

- Regular feedback and data-driven assessments enhance performance.

7. Mobile Apps:

- Mobile devices allow employees to manage work hours on the go.

- Apps for time tracking, calendar management and task prioritization enhance productivity.

8. Well-Defined Policies:

- Employers must set clear expectations regarding technology use during work hours.

- Balancing connectivity with reasonable working hours is essential

Technology empowers individuals and organizations to manage work hours efficiently, leading to improved productivity and work-life balance. Implementing technology for work hour management brings both benefits and challenges. However, with the right tools and well-defined policies in place, employees can effectively navigate these challenges. By utilizing apps for time tracking, calendar management and task prioritization, workers can better manage their time and stay organized, ultimately increasing their productivity. Additionally, employers must establish clear expectations around technology use during work hours to ensure a healthy balance between connectivity and downtime. Overall, technology can be a valuable tool in helping individuals and organizations optimize their work hours and achieve a better work-life balance.

However, it is important for employers to also recognize the potential downsides of technology in the workplace. Constant connectivity can lead to burnout and decreased job satisfaction if employees feel pressure to always be available. It is crucial for organizations to foster a culture that encourages employees to unplug and take breaks when needed. By promoting a healthy work-life balance, employers can help prevent employee fatigue and improve overall job performance. Additionally, providing training on digital wellness and stress management can help employees better cope with the demands of the modern workplace. Ultimately, finding the right balance between utilizing technology for productivity and maintaining personal well-being is key to creating a positive and sustainable work environment.

Challenges

Let's explore some of the common challenges:

1.   Cost of Technology and Implementation:

- While technology can bring many benefits to HR management, there are costs associated with its implementation. Organizations need to invest in software, hardware, training and ongoing maintenance.

- Balancing the upfront costs with long-term gains is essential.

2.   Resistance to Change and Adoption:

- Employees may resist adopting new technology due to familiarity with existing processes or fear of job displacement.

- Change management strategies are crucial to encourage acceptance and smooth adoption.

3.   Data Privacy and Security Concerns:

- Storing employee data electronically raises privacy and security issues.

- Organizations must ensure compliance with data protection regulations and safeguard sensitive information.

4. Seamless Integration with Existing Systems:

- Integrating new technology with legacy HR systems can be challenging.

- Ensuring compatibility and data flow between different platforms is critical.

5. Maintaining Data Accuracy and Quality:

- Automated systems rely on accurate data. Inaccurate or outdated information can lead to errors.

- Regular data audits and quality checks are necessary.

6. Potential for Bias and Discrimination:

- Algorithms used in technology may inadvertently perpetuate biases present in historical data.

- Organizations must actively monitor and address bias to ensure fair treatment.

7.   Impact on Job Roles and Responsibilities:

- Automation can change job roles. Some tasks previously done manually may become obsolete.

- Reskilling employees and redefining roles are essential.

8.   User Experience and Training:

- Employees need proper training to use new technology effectively.

- A user-friendly interface and ongoing support are crucial for successful adoption.

Organizations must navigate these challenges to fully realize the potential of technology in work hour management.

It is important for organizations to prioritize employee training and support in order to ensure a smooth transition to new technology. This will not only improve user experience but also increase efficiency and productivity in the workplace. By addressing these challenges, businesses can effectively harness the benefits of technology in managing work hours while also ensuring fair treatment and the successful evolution of job roles.

This can ultimately lead to a more streamlined and effective work hour management system, benefiting both employees and employers alike. In addition, proper training and support can also help to mitigate any resistance or pushback from employees who may be hesitant to embrace new technology. By investing in the necessary resources and support, organizations can create a culture of continuous learning and improvement, ultimately leading to a more efficient and productive workforce. It is essential for organizations to stay proactive and adaptable in the face of technological advancements, in order to stay competitive and meet the evolving needs of the modern workplace.

In developing nations, managing working hours presents several complex challenges. These challenges may include cultural norms surrounding work hours, lack of access to technology for tracking hours and limited resources for implementing flexible work arrangements. However, by addressing these challenges head-on and implementing strategies to improve time management and productivity, organizations in developing nations can create a more efficient and effective workforce. This can lead to increased economic growth and a better quality of life for employees. By investing in technology and training programs, organizations can help employees better track their working hours and make informed decisions about their schedules. Additionally, promoting a culture of work-life balance and offering flexible work arrangements can improve employee satisfaction and retention. Ultimately, by overcoming the obstacles related to managing working hours, businesses in developing nations can boost productivity, increase profitability and contribute to overall societal advancement. For example, a manufacturing company in a developing nation implemented an automated time tracking system for their employees, allowing them to accurately record their hours and receive fair compensation. This led to increased efficiency in production processes and higher employee morale, resulting in reduced turnover rates and improved overall performance for the company.

As a result, the company was able to meet customer demands more effectively, expand their market reach and ultimately grow their business. This success story highlights the transformative impact that effective time management can have on businesses in developing nations, demonstrating the potential for sustainable growth and economic development. Additionally, by ensuring fair compensation and transparent tracking of working hours, businesses can also promote social responsibility and ethical practices within their operations. This not only benefits employees by providing them with a stable and supportive work environment, but also enhances the company's reputation and relationships with stakeholders in the global marketplace. Overall, prioritizing effective time management is not only essential for business success, but also for driving positive change and progress in developing nations. By empowering employees to manage their time efficiently, businesses can increase productivity and innovation, leading to further growth and competitiveness in the market. This approach can also contribute to reducing poverty and inequality by creating more job opportunities and fostering sustainable economic growth.

CHAPTER-3

Gross Manufacturing Value Added (GMVA)

@dibyenduchoudhury

Chapter 3: Gross Manufacturing Value Added (GMVA)

Improving Gross Manufacturing Value Added (GMVA) for a nation can be a complex process that involves various factors. These factors can include investment in technology and infrastructure, enhancing the skills and education of the workforce, streamlining production processes and promoting innovation within the manufacturing sector. Additionally, creating a business-friendly environment, reducing bureaucratic red tape and implementing supportive government policies can also contribute to improving GMVA. By addressing these factors effectively, a nation can boost its manufacturing sector's contribution to the overall economy and increase its competitiveness in the global market. This can lead to higher productivity, increased job opportunities and ultimately, economic growth. It is essential for governments and businesses to work together to create an environment that fosters continuous improvement and sustainable development in the manufacturing industry.

This collaboration can involve providing training and education programs to upskill the workforce, investing in research and development to drive innovation and promoting sustainable practices to minimize environmental impact. By working together, governments and businesses can create a thriving manufacturing sector that not only benefits the economy but also enhances the quality of life for citizens. Additionally, fostering a culture of collaboration and partnership can lead to greater efficiency, cost savings and overall success in the manufacturing industry. Ultimately, by prioritizing GMVA and working together towards common goals, nations can position themselves as leaders in the global marketplace and drive long-term economic prosperity. For example, a country may implement regulations requiring manufacturers to use renewable energy sources and reduce waste in their production processes. This collaboration between government and businesses can lead to the development of innovative technologies and practices that not only benefit the environment but also boost competitiveness in the global market. Additionally, by sharing knowledge and resources, companies can streamline operations, reduce costs and ultimately improve their bottom line while contributing to a more sustainable future.

However, in some cases, strict regulations can stifle innovation and hinder economic growth. For instance, if a country imposes too many restrictions on businesses, they may struggle to adapt and invest in new technologies, leading to a decline in competitiveness and overall economic prosperity.

On the other hand, striking a balance between regulation and innovation is crucial for fostering sustainable development. By implementing smart regulations that encourage eco-friendly practices without stifling creativity, businesses can thrive while also protecting the environment. This approach not only benefits companies in the long run but also ensures a healthier planet for future generations. Ultimately, it is essential for policymakers to work closely with businesses to create a regulatory framework that promotes innovation and sustainability hand in hand.

How to Improve GMVA

Here are some ways that can help improve GMVA:

1. **Investing in technology:** Investing in new technologies can help increase the efficiency of the manufacturing process, reduce costs and improve the quality of products. For example, a manufacturing company could invest in renewable energy sources to power their factories, reducing their carbon footprint and operating costs. Additionally, implementing sustainable supply chain practices, such as sourcing materials from eco-friendly suppliers, can help reduce waste and promote environmental stewardship within the industry.

2. **Improving infrastructure:** Improving infrastructure such as roads, ports and airports can help reduce transportation costs and improve the supply chain, which can lead to increased productivity and competitiveness. Furthermore, investing in infrastructure improvements can also enhance connectivity and accessibility, making it

easier for businesses to reach new markets and customers. By expanding and modernizing transportation networks, companies can streamline their operations and expedite the delivery of goods, ultimately boosting overall efficiency and profitability. Overall, prioritizing infrastructure development is crucial for creating a more resilient and sustainable business environment that can support long-term growth and success. For example, a company that invests in upgrading its distribution network by implementing new technology and expanding its transportation routes can significantly reduce delivery times and costs. This can lead to increased customer satisfaction and loyalty, as well as a competitive edge in the market against other businesses that have not made similar investments in infrastructure improvements.

3. Providing training and education: Providing training and education to the workforce can help improve their skills and knowledge, which can lead to increased productivity and innovation. In addition, investing in employee development can also boost morale and job satisfaction, leading to higher retention rates and a more engaged workforce. By continuously investing in training and education, companies can stay ahead of industry trends and ensure that their employees are equipped to handle new challenges and opportunities. Ultimately, this can result in a more efficient and effective organization that is better positioned for long-term success. For example, a company that provides regular training and development opportunities for its employees may see an increase in the adoption of new technologies and practices, leading to improved efficiency and competitiveness in the market. Additionally, employees who feel supported in their professional growth are more likely to be motivated and engaged in their work, contributing to a positive company culture and overall success.

4. Encouraging innovation: Encouraging innovation through research and development can help create new products and processes, which can lead to increased competitiveness and growth. By investing in research and development, companies can stay ahead of the curve and anticipate market trends, giving them a competitive edge. This focus on innovation can also attract top talent who are eager to work for a company that values creativity and forward thinking. Overall, fostering a culture of innovation can be a key driver in long-term success and sustainability for any organization. For example, a tech company like Apple invests heavily in research and development to create innovative products like the iPhone and iPad, which have helped them become a leader in the industry. This focus on innovation has not only driven their success but also attracted top engineers and designers who are excited to work on cutting-edge technology.

5. Promoting exports: Promoting exports can help increase demand for domestically produced goods, which can lead to increased production and economic growth. Investing in research and development can also lead to the creation of new products and services that can be exported to other countries, further increasing revenue and market share. By focusing on innovation and constantly improving their offerings, companies can stay ahead of the competition and continue to grow their business globally. In today's highly competitive market, staying innovative and adaptable is crucial for long-term success and sustainability. For example, a company that specializes in renewable energy technology could invest in research and development to create new, more efficient products. By exporting these innovative products to other countries, they can not only increase their revenue but also contribute to the global effort towards sustainability. This can ultimately lead to increased production, economic growth and a stronger position in the market compared to competitors who are not as focused on innovation.

Sustainable Practices

By adopting sustainable practices such as using renewable energy sources and reducing waste, businesses can minimize their environmental impact while also saving money in the long term. Collaborating with suppliers: Working with suppliers who share the same commitment to sustainability can help businesses create a more sustainable supply chain and reduce their carbon footprint. By implementing these strategies, businesses can achieve both economic success and environmental responsibility, setting a positive example for others in the industry.

These are just some of the ways that can help improve GMVA for a nation. Implementing sustainable practices not only benefits the environment but also contributes to the overall well-being of society. By prioritizing sustainability, businesses can create a positive impact on their communities and inspire others to follow suit. It is crucial for businesses to take a proactive approach in addressing environmental issues and work towards a more sustainable future for all. By making a commitment to sustainability, businesses can reduce their carbon footprint, conserve resources and protect natural habitats. This not only enhances their reputation and attracts environmentally-conscious consumers but also fosters a sense of social responsibility. Ultimately, by integrating sustainable practices into their operations, businesses can play a significant role in shaping a greener, healthier future for generations to come. It is imperative for businesses to recognize the importance of sustainability and take action to preserve the planet for future generations. For example, a clothing company that commits to using recycled materials in their products and implementing energy-efficient manufacturing processes can significantly reduce their environmental impact. By doing so, they not only appeal to eco-conscious consumers but also set a positive example for other businesses in the industry to follow suit.

However, not all businesses prioritize sustainability and some may continue to exploit natural resources and contribute to pollution without regard for the future. For instance, a mining company that disregards environmental regulations and continues to extract resources without considering the long-term consequences can have devastating effects on local ecosystems and communities.

Balanced Gross
Manufacturing Value
Added Growth (GMVA)
Chapter-4
YOU MEAN TO SAY
NATURAL RESOURCES ARE NOT
ENOUGH FOR ECONOMIC GROWTH
@dibyenduchoudhury

Chapter 4. Balanced Gross Manufacturing Value Added Growth (GMVA)

Is It More Important Than Anything Else?

Gross Manufacturing Value Added (GMVA) refers to the value of output from the manufacturing sector minus the value of intermediate inputs. It is a crucial indicator of the economic health and performance of a nation's manufacturing sector. While GMVA growth is undeniably important, especially for a developing nation, asserting that it is more important than anything else can be overly simplistic. This section of the chapter explores the significance of GMVA growth, its role in economic development and the need to balance it with other critical aspects of a comprehensive economic strategy. GMVA growth is often used as a measure of industrial productivity and competitiveness, as it reflects the sector's ability to add value to raw materials and inputs. However, focusing solely on GMVA growth can overlook other important factors such as job creation, income distribution and environmental sustainability. A holistic approach to economic development requires balancing GMVA growth with policies that promote inclusive growth, sustainable practices and social well-being. Ultimately, a nation's manufacturing sector should strive for sustainable growth that benefits the economy as a whole, rather than focusing solely on increasing GMVA. For example, a country may experience high GMVA growth in its manufacturing sector due to its heavy reliance on unsustainable practices like deforestation and the exploitation of low-wage labour. This may lead to short-term economic gains but also contribute to long-term environmental degradation and social inequalities. Thus, a narrow focus on GMVA growth without considering broader impacts can result in a counterproductive and unsustainable development path.

The Significance of GMVA Growth

Economic Growth and Industrialization

GMVA growth is a key driver of economic growth and industrialization. Manufacturing sectors typically offer higher productivity levels compared to agriculture and provide a pathway for economies to diversify and reduce their dependence on volatile primary sectors. For developing countries, rapid industrialization driven by manufacturing can lead to significant economic transformation, a higher GDP and improved living standards. However, it is important to note that GMVA growth must be managed carefully to avoid negative consequences such as environmental degradation, resource depletion and social inequality. Sustainable industrialization practices, including the use of clean technologies and responsible resource management, are essential to ensuring that GMVA growth benefits all sectors of society in the long term. Additionally, policies that promote inclusive growth, support small and medium enterprises and invest in human capital are crucial for maximizing the positive impacts of GMVA growth on economic development.

For instance, China's impressive economic growth over the past few decades has largely been a result of strong growth in its manufacturing sector. By focusing on manufacturing, China was able to lift millions out of poverty, create a substantial middle class and become a global economic powerhouse. However, this growth has also led to significant environmental degradation, income inequality and social unrest. Despite the overall economic success, many rural areas in China have been left behind and continue to struggle with poverty and a lack of access to basic services. This highlights the importance of ensuring that GMVA growth is inclusive and sustainable in order to truly benefit all sectors of society in the long term. In order to address these challenges, China has implemented various policies and initiatives aimed at promoting sustainable development and reducing inequality. These efforts include investing in renewable energy, improving access to education and healthcare in rural areas and promoting inclusive economic growth. By placing a higher priority on these goals, China can guarantee that all members of society benefit from its economic growth, resulting in a more prosperous and secure future for the whole nation. It is crucial for China to continue to prioritize inclusive and sustainable growth in order to address the disparities that exist within its society and create a more equitable and prosperous future for all of its citizens.

But because the press and media are tightly controlled, we are unable to access a large amount of China's real-time data and verify their claims with actual data. This lack of transparency in China's media poses a challenge to accurately assessing the effectiveness of their policies towards inclusive and sustainable growth. Without access to reliable data, it is difficult to determine whether the government's priorities are truly benefiting all members of society. In order to ensure that China's economic growth is truly inclusive and sustainable, it is essential for the government to increase transparency and allow for independent verification of their progress towards these goals. By doing so, China can build trust with its citizens and the international community and pave the way for a more prosperous and equitable future for all.

Employment Generation

The manufacturing sector is a significant source of employment. As it grows, it creates a wide range of job opportunities, from low-skilled to high-skilled positions. This is particularly crucial for developing countries with large, young populations. For instance, India's "Make in India" initiative aims to boost manufacturing to create jobs and absorb the large number of new entrants into the labour market each year. By investing in manufacturing and creating more job opportunities, China can also address issues of income inequality and poverty within its own borders. A strong manufacturing sector can provide stable and well-paying jobs for millions of people, lifting them out of poverty and improving their standard of living. Furthermore, by focusing on environmentally sustainable practices and technologies in manufacturing, China can also demonstrate its commitment to addressing global challenges such as climate change. This combination of economic growth, social development and environmental stewardship will not only benefit China but also contribute to a more stable and prosperous world for all.

Export Earnings and Trade Balance

Manufacturing industries often produce goods that are traded internationally, contributing to export earnings and improving the trade balance. A strong manufacturing sector can help reduce trade deficits by increasing exports and substituting imports with domestically produced goods. South Korea's economic strategy, which focused on developing a competitive manufacturing sector, significantly improved its trade balance and economic stability. By prioritizing stewardship and sustainability in manufacturing practices, China can not only boost its export earnings but also enhance its global reputation as a responsible economic player. This will not only benefit the country economically but also contribute to a more sustainable and prosperous world for all. Taking a cue from South Korea's success, China can work towards a more balanced trade relationship with other countries by prioritizing the development of a competitive manufacturing sector that focuses on sustainability and innovation. Ultimately, this shift towards responsible manufacturing practices will not only benefit China but also have a positive impact on the global economy and environment.

Several Western countries have used African countries, including Ghana and Nigeria, as dumping grounds for electronics garbage, automobiles and other items over the past decade. China dumped goods and their landed prices were far lower than manufacturing costs, destroying small and medium-sized businesses in targeted countries. There are numerous approaches to defending the national market, including antidumping laws, trade barriers, tariffs and nontariff barriers. In such cases, national regulatory and monitoring organizations should be on high alert. They must closely monitor imports and exports to ensure that unfair competition and dumping practices do not harm local industries. Additionally, cooperation between African countries is crucial in order to collectively combat this issue and protect their economies. Strengthening regulations and enforcing penalties for those who engage in dumping practices is essential to safeguarding the economic interests of African nations. By taking a united stand against these harmful practices, African countries can work towards creating a fair and sustainable trading environment for all. For example, if a foreign company floods the market with cheap goods below market value, it can drive local producers out of business. This not only threatens the livelihoods of workers in those industries but also weakens the overall economy of the country. By working together to enforce regulations and penalties against such practices, African nations can protect their industries and promote fair competition.

This can help to ensure that local businesses have a level playing field and are able to thrive in the global market. Additionally, by standing together, African nations can also negotiate better trade deals with foreign partners, ensuring that they are not taken advantage of in international trade agreements. By prioritizing the interests of their own industries and workers, African countries can work towards economic growth and development that benefits their people as a whole. Ultimately, unity and cooperation among African nations can lead to a more prosperous and sustainable future for the continent.

Limitations of Focusing Solely on GMVA Growth

Sustainable Development

While GMVA growth is vital, focusing exclusively on it can lead to environmental degradation and unsustainable practices. Manufacturing processes can be resource-intensive and polluting, contributing to issues such as air and water pollution, deforestation and climate change. Therefore, it is essential to balance manufacturing growth with sustainable practices to ensure long-term environmental health. This can be achieved through the implementation of green technologies, renewable energy sources and waste reduction strategies. Additionally, investing in education and training programs can help develop a skilled workforce that is equipped to adopt sustainable practices in the manufacturing sector. By prioritizing sustainable development alongside GMVA growth, African nations can build a resilient economy that benefits both current and future generations.

Inclusive Growth

GMVA growth does not automatically translate into inclusive growth. The benefits of manufacturing-led growth can be unevenly distributed, leading to regional disparities and social inequality. Policies must ensure that the growth of the manufacturing sector benefits a broad spectrum of society, including marginalized and vulnerable populations. This can be achieved through targeted policies such as skills thraining programs, job creation initiatives and social protection schemes. By ensuring that the benefits of manufacturing-led growth are shared equitably, African nations can create a more inclusive economy that lifts people out of poverty and fosters social cohesion.

Ultimately, inclusive growth in the manufacturing sector will not only drive economic development but also contribute to the overall well-being and stability of society.

Diversification and innovation

An overemphasis on manufacturing can overshadow other critical sectors, such as services and agriculture. A balanced economy requires diversification to mitigate risks and foster innovation. For instance, while manufacturing has been a cornerstone of Germany's economy, the country also boasts a strong services sector and a focus on technological innovation, contributing to its overall economic resilience. This diversification has allowed Germany to weather economic downturns in the manufacturing sector and maintain stability. Furthermore, innovation in various sectors has led to the creation of new jobs and opportunities for growth. Therefore, a balanced economy that values diversification and innovation across multiple sectors is essential for long-term sustainable development and societal well-being. For example, Germany's automotive industry faced challenges during the global financial crisis, but the country's strong services sector and focus on technological innovation helped offset losses and maintain economic stability. Additionally, the growth of renewable energy technology in Germany has created new jobs and opportunities for sustainable development, further demonstrating the benefits of a diversified and innovative economy.

Balancing GMVA Growth with Other Priorities

To harness the full potential of GMVA growth, it is essential to integrate it into a broader economic strategy that addresses sustainability, inclusivity and diversification. Here are a few key considerations:

Sustainable Practices

Implementing green manufacturing practices and investing in clean technologies can help reduce the environmental impact of industrial growth. Policies promoting energy efficiency, waste reduction and the use of renewable resources can ensure that manufacturing growth is sustainable. Inclusivity and Diversity Prioritizing inclusivity and diversity in the workforce can help ensure that the benefits of GMVA growth are shared among all members of society. This can involve creating opportunities for underrepresented groups, promoting equal pay and advancement opportunities and fostering a culture of diversity and inclusion within the manufacturing sector. By embracing diversity, companies can tap into a wider talent pool and drive innovation and creativity. Overall, a focus on inclusivity can lead to a more equitable distribution of economic benefits and a more resilient and dynamic economy.

Skill Development and Education

Investing in education and vocational training is crucial to ensure that the workforce can meet the demands of a growing manufacturing sector. Skill development programs can enhance labour productivity and ensure that workers can adapt to technological advancements in manufacturing. Additionally, providing opportunities for continued education and training can lead to upward mobility for employees within the industry. By investing in the development of a skilled workforce, companies can also improve their competitiveness in the global market. Ultimately, a focus on skill development and education can help to drive economic growth and prosperity within the manufacturing sector. For example, a manufacturing company in the automotive industry may implement a training program for its employees to learn new technologies such as robotics and automation. This will not only improve the efficiency of their production processes but also help employees advance in their careers within the company.

Innovation and R&D

Encouraging research and development (R&D) in manufacturing can drive innovation, improve competitiveness and lead to the creation of high-value products. Government incentives and support for R&D activities can foster a culture of innovation within the manufacturing sector.

Social Equity

Policies that promote fair wages, worker rights and social protections can ensure that the benefits of GMVA growth are widely shared. Addressing regional disparities and investing in infrastructure in underdeveloped areas can promote more balanced economic growth. Sustainability and Environmental Responsibility Implementing sustainable practices in manufacturing, such as reducing waste and greenhouse gas emissions, can help mitigate the environmental impact of industrial activities. Embracing renewable energy sources and eco-friendly technologies can contribute to a cleaner and healthier future for all. By prioritizing sustainability, companies can not only protect the planet but also enhance their reputation and appeal to environmentally conscious consumers.

While GMVA growth is undeniably important for economic development, asserting that it is more important than anything else overlooks the complexities of sustainable and inclusive growth. A balanced approach that integrates GMVA growth with sustainable practices, skill development, innovation and social equity is essential for long-term economic prosperity. By adopting such a holistic strategy, nations can ensure that the growth of their manufacturing sector contributes to overall economic health and the well-being of their populations. This approach not only benefits the environment but also fosters a more stable and resilient economy. Investing in sustainable practices, skill development and innovation can lead to greater efficiency, cost savings and a competitive edge in the global market. Furthermore, promoting social equity ensures that the benefits of GMVA growth are shared equitably among all members of society, reducing inequalities and improving overall quality of life. By prioritizing these factors alongside economic growth, nations can create a more sustainable and inclusive future for all.

CHAPTER-5

GOVERNMENT OF INDIA'S INITIATIVES TO IMPROVE GROSS MANUFACTURING VALUE ADDED (GMVA)

Chapter 5: Government of India's Initiatives to Improve Gross Manufacturing Value Added (GMVA)

The Government of India has recognized the pivotal role of manufacturing in driving economic growth, creating employment and improving living standards. In pursuit of enhancing Gross Manufacturing Value Added (GMVA), the government has launched several schemes and initiatives aimed at boosting the manufacturing sector. This essay explores the importance of GMVA, discusses various schemes introduced by the Government of India and analyzes their potential impact on the country's manufacturing landscape. One example of such initiative is the "Make in India" campaign, which aims to attract foreign investment and promote domestic manufacturing. Another example is the Production Linked Incentive (PLI) scheme, which incentivizes manufacturers to increase production and invest in new technologies to improve GMVA.

The Importance of GMVA

Gross Manufacturing Value Added (GMVA) is a critical indicator of the health of a nation's manufacturing sector. It measures the net output of manufacturing activities by subtracting the value of intermediate inputs from the total value of manufacturing output. Improving GMVA is essential for several reasons:

1. **Economic Growth:** A robust manufacturing sector contributes significantly to GDP, fostering economic development.
2. **Employment Generation:** Manufacturing creates numerous jobs, providing employment opportunities for a large segment of the population.
3. **Trade Balance:** A strong manufacturing sector can boost exports and reduce dependence on imports, improving the trade balance.
4. **Technological Advancement:** Manufacturing drives technological innovation and the adoption of new technologies.

5. Regional Development: Manufacturing can stimulate regional development by establishing industries in less developed areas.

Key Government Schemes to Improve GMVA

The Government of India has launched several schemes and initiatives to enhance GMVA, focusing on various aspects such as infrastructure development, skill enhancement, technological innovation and financial support. Some of the prominent schemes include:

1. Make in India

Objective: Launched in September 2014, the Make in India initiative aims to transform India into a global manufacturing hub by encouraging both multinational and domestic companies to manufacture their products in India.

Key Features:

- Sectoral Focus: The initiative identifies 25 key sectors, including automobiles, pharmaceuticals, textiles and electronics and provides targeted support to these sectors.

- Ease of Doing Business: Simplification of procedures and regulations to make it easier to start and operate businesses in India.

- FDI Liberalization: Liberalization of Foreign Direct Investment (FDI) policies to attract foreign investment in the manufacturing sector.

- Innovation and R&D: Promotion of innovation and research and development through various incentives and support mechanisms.

Impact:

Make in India has attracted significant investments and led to the establishment of numerous manufacturing facilities across the country. For example, the initiative has encouraged global electronics companies like Apple and Samsung to set up manufacturing units in India.

2. Production-Linked Incentive (PLI) Scheme

Objective: The PLI scheme aims to boost domestic manufacturing and attract large-scale investments in key sectors by providing financial incentives linked to production and performance.

Key Features:

- Sector-Specific Incentives: The scheme covers multiple sectors, including electronics, pharmaceuticals, automobiles and textiles, offering incentives based on incremental sales and investments.

- Job Creation: Encourages the creation of jobs by incentivizing large-scale manufacturing operations.

- Export Promotion: Supports the enhancement of manufacturing capacities for export-oriented production.

Impact:

The PLI scheme has already shown positive results, with substantial investments committed in sectors such as electronics and pharmaceuticals. For instance, the scheme has led to the establishment of new manufacturing units by companies like

Foxconn and Wistron, contributing to the growth of India's electronics manufacturing sector.

3. Atmanirbhar Bharat Abhiyan (Self-Reliant India Campaign)

Objective: Launched in response to the COVID-19 pandemic, the Atmanirbhar Bharat Abhiyan aims to make India self-reliant by boosting domestic manufacturing and reducing dependence on imports.

Key Features:

- Financial Support: Provision of financial packages to support various sectors, including MSMEs, agriculture and manufacturing.

- Infrastructure Development: Investment in infrastructure projects to enhance manufacturing capabilities.

- Supply Chain Resilience: Strengthening supply chains to ensure the availability of raw materials and components for manufacturing.

Impact:

The campaign has led to increased investment in critical sectors and has encouraged the localization of supply chains. For example, the defense manufacturing sector has seen significant growth, with increased production of indigenous defense equipment.

4. National Manufacturing Policy (NMP)

Objective: The NMP aims to increase the share of manufacturing in GDP to 25% and create 100 million jobs by 2022.

Key Features:

- National Investment and Manufacturing Zones (NIMZs): Establishment of large industrial townships with world-class infrastructure and regulatory support.

- Skill Development: Initiatives to enhance the skills of the workforce to meet the demands of the manufacturing sector.

- Technology Acquisition and Development Fund (TADF): Support for the acquisition and development of advanced technologies.

Impact:

The NMP has facilitated the development of industrial clusters and NIMZs, which have attracted significant investments and boosted manufacturing activities. For example, the Delhi-Mumbai Industrial Corridor (DMIC) is a flagship project under the NMP that aims to create a global manufacturing and investment destination.

5. Skill India Mission

Objective: Launched in 2015, the Skill India Mission aims to equip the workforce with the skills required for various sectors, including manufacturing, to enhance productivity and employability.

Key Features:

- Pradhan Mantri Kaushal Vikas Yojana (PMKVY): A flagship scheme under the Skill India Mission that provides short-term skill training and certification programs.

- Industry Partnerships: Collaboration with industry partners to design and implement training programs that meet industry needs.

- Skill Development Centers: Establishment of training centers across the country to provide skill development opportunities.

Impact:

The Skill India Mission has trained millions of individuals, enhanced their employability and contributed to the growth of the manufacturing sector. For instance, the automotive and electronics sectors have benefited from a skilled workforce trained under this mission.

6. Smart Cities Mission

Objective: Launched in 2015, the Smart Cities Mission aims to develop 100 smart cities across India to improve the quality of life and create an enabling environment for economic activities, including manufacturing.

Key Features:

- Infrastructure Development: Development of modern infrastructure, including transportation, energy and communication systems.

-       Sustainable Practices: Emphasis on sustainability and the use of smart technologies to enhance resource efficiency.

-       Industrial Clusters: Integration of industrial clusters within smart cities to boost manufacturing activities.

Impact:

The Smart Cities Mission has led to the development of world-class infrastructure, which has attracted investments in manufacturing and other sectors. For example, the Pune Smart City project has enhanced the city's infrastructure, making it an attractive destination for manufacturing companies.

Challenges and Recommendations

While the aforementioned schemes have shown promising results, there are several challenges that need to be addressed to maximize their impact on GMVA:

Challenges

1.   Regulatory Hurdles: Despite improvements, regulatory complexities and

bureaucratic red tape continue to pose challenges for businesses.

2. Infrastructure Deficits: Inadequate infrastructure in certain regions hampers manufacturing activities and increases costs.

3. Skill Gaps: There remains a mismatch between the skills possessed by the workforce and the requirements of the manufacturing sector.

4. Access to Finance: Small and medium-sized enterprises (SMEs) often face difficulties in accessing affordable finance for expansion and modernization.

5. Technological Lag: Many manufacturing units, especially in traditional sectors, lag in adopting advanced technologies and automation.

Recommendations

1. Regulatory Reforms: Streamline regulations and procedures further to reduce compliance costs and enhance the ease of doing business.

2.   Infrastructure Investment: Continue to invest in transportation, energy and digital infrastructure, particularly in underdeveloped regions, to support manufacturing growth.

3. Skill Development: Expand and intensify skill development initiatives to bridge the skill gap, focusing on emerging technologies and advanced manufacturing techniques.

4.   Financial Support: Enhance access to finance for SMEs through targeted schemes, credit guarantees and interest subsidies.

5.   Technology Adoption: Promote the adoption of Industry 4.0 technologies through incentives, subsidies and technical assistance programs.

The Government of India has undertaken several schemes and initiatives to promote the manufacturing sector in the country. Some of the major initiatives include:

1. Make in India initiative: This initiative aims to promote domestic manufacturing and attract foreign investment in the country.

2. Industrial Corridor Development Programme: This program aims to develop industrial corridors across the country to promote manufacturing and create employment opportunities.

3. Ease of Doing Business: The government has implemented several reforms to improve the ease of doing business in the country, which can help attract more investment and promote growth.

4. National Single Window System: This system aims to simplify the process of obtaining clearances and approvals for setting up a business in the country.

5. PM Gati Shakti National Master Plan (NMP): This plan aims to develop a multi-modal transportation system to improve connectivity and reduce logistics costs.

6. National Logistics Policy: This policy aims to create a single-window e-logistics market and improve the efficiency of the logistics sector.

7. Indian Footwear and Leather Development Programme (IFLDP): This programme aims to promote the development of the footwear and leather industry in the country.

These initiatives can help improve the Gross Manufacturing Value Added (GMVA) of the country by promoting domestic manufacturing, attracting foreign investment and improving the ease of doing business. However, it's important to note that the effectiveness of these initiatives can vary depending on the specific circumstances of each industry and region.

The Government of India has undertaken numerous initiatives to improve Gross Manufacturing Value Added (GMVA), recognizing the critical role of manufacturing in driving economic growth and development. Schemes such as Make in India, the Production-Linked Incentive (PLI) scheme, Atmanirbhar Bharat Abhiyan, the National Manufacturing Policy (NMP), the Skill India Mission and the Smart Cities Mission are pivotal in enhancing manufacturing capabilities, creating employment opportunities and fostering technological innovation. These initiatives aim to boost the competitiveness of Indian manufacturers on a global scale and attract foreign investment in the sector. By focusing on skill development, infrastructure enhancement and policy reforms, the government is laying the foundation for a vibrant and sustainable manufacturing ecosystem in the country. With continued support and implementation of these programs, India is poised to emerge as a major player in the global manufacturing landscape, driving economic growth and prosperity for its citizens.

While these initiatives have shown significant progress, addressing challenges related to regulatory hurdles, infrastructure deficits, skill gaps, access to finance and technological lag is essential to maximize their impact. By implementing targeted reforms and fostering a conducive environment for manufacturing, India can achieve substantial improvements in GMVA, paving the way for sustainable and inclusive economic growth. Continued investment in research and development, innovation and upskilling of the workforce will be crucial in ensuring that India remains competitive in the global market. Additionally, streamlining bureaucratic processes and improving access to financing for small and medium-sized enterprises will help create a more vibrant and dynamic manufacturing sector. By taking these steps, India can solidify its position as a powerhouse in the global manufacturing industry and provide meaningful opportunities for its growing population.

In conclusion, the Government of India's concerted efforts to boost GMVA through a comprehensive set of schemes and policies demonstrate a strategic commitment to transforming the manufacturing sector. These initiatives, coupled with continued reforms and investments, can position India as a global manufacturing powerhouse, driving long-term economic prosperity and development. Furthermore, by fostering innovation and technology adoption in the manufacturing sector, India can enhance its competitiveness and attract foreign investment. This will not only create more job opportunities but also boost the overall economic growth of the country. With a strong focus on sustainability and efficiency, India has the potential to become a leader in the global manufacturing landscape, setting an example for other emerging economies to follow. For example, by investing in renewable energy technologies and implementing sustainable practices in manufacturing processes, India can reduce its carbon footprint and contribute to global efforts to mitigate climate change. Additionally, by leveraging advanced technologies such as artificial intelligence and automation, Indian manufacturers can improve productivity and quality standards, making them more attractive to international markets.

Government initiatives like Green Clusters, RAMP (Raising and Amplifying the MSME Performance), Surya Mitra and others are boosting the renewable energy sector. These initiatives aim to promote the adoption of renewable energy sources and increase the efficiency of power generation in India. By supporting these programs and investing in renewable energy projects, India can further reduce its dependence on fossil fuels and decrease greenhouse gas emissions. This shift towards clean energy will not only benefit the environment but also create new job opportunities and drive economic growth in the country. In the long run, India's commitment to sustainability and innovation will position it as a leader in the global market for clean energy technologies.

You Can
Do It !

CHAPTER-6

Achievement
Motivation and
Employee
Motivation:
Understanding Their
Impact on
Individuals

@dibyenduchoudhury

Chapter 6: Achievement Motivation and Employee Motivation: Understanding Their Impact on Individuals

Achievement motivation and employee motivation are two distinct yet interconnected concepts that play significant roles in shaping individual behaviour and performance in the workplace. While achievement motivation focuses on the personal drive to excel and succeed, employee motivation pertains to the factors that influence an individual's willingness and enthusiasm to perform effectively in their job. Understanding these concepts is essential for employers and leaders to create a work environment that fosters both individual and organizational success. By recognizing and nurturing employees' achievement motivation, employers can tap into their drive to excel and reach their full potential. Similarly, by understanding and addressing factors that influence employee motivation, such as recognition, rewards and a positive work culture, leaders can create a supportive and motivating environment that encourages high performance. Ultimately, fostering both achievement and employee motivation can lead to increased productivity, job satisfaction and overall success for both individuals and the organization as a whole. For example, a company that implements a recognition program where employees are publicly acknowledged for their hard work and achievements can boost morale and motivation. Additionally, offering incentives such as bonuses or promotions for top performers can further incentivize employees to strive for excellence.

Prof. David McLeland developed the Achievement Motivation Theory and tested it in three countries, including India. In India, he sought the support of Ni-msme (then SIET) in Kakinada Andhra Pradesh, with the Fisherman Community. Through his research and collaboration with Ni-msme and the Fisherman Community in India, Prof. McLeland was able to observe how different cultures and backgrounds can influence motivation and achievement. By understanding the unique factors that drive individuals in different settings, organizations can tailor their motivational strategies to better suit their employees' needs. This cross-cultural approach to motivation can ultimately lead to a more engaged and productive workforce, benefiting both the employees and the organization as a whole. For example, Prof. McLeland found that the Fisherman Community in India valued communal support and recognition from their peers as a key motivator for their work. By incorporating these elements into their motivational strategies, organizations can foster a sense of community and collaboration among employees, leading to increased job satisfaction and productivity. This tailored approach can also help bridge cultural gaps and promote diversity and inclusion within the workplace.

By recognizing and valuing the unique motivators of different cultural groups, organizations can create a more inclusive and supportive environment for all employees. This not only enhances employee morale and engagement, but also helps to attract and retain a diverse workforce. In addition, by promoting diversity and inclusion, organizations can benefit from a wider range of perspectives and ideas, leading to innovation and creativity in the workplace. Ultimately, by tailoring motivational strategies to the specific needs and values of different cultural groups, organizations can create a more harmonious and productive work environment for all employees.

Differences in Motivation

Achievement motivation is characterized by a strong desire to set and achieve challenging goals, often driven by internal rewards such as a sense of accomplishment or personal growth. Individuals with high achievement motivation are often self-starters who seek out challenges and are willing to take risks to achieve their objectives. On the other hand, employee motivation encompasses a broader range of factors, including job satisfaction, recognition, rewards and a positive work environment. While achievement motivation is more intrinsic and self-directed, both intrinsic and extrinsic factors, such as the organization's culture and the nature of the work itself, can affect employee motivation. Ultimately, a combination of achievement motivation and employee motivation can drive individuals to excel in their roles and contribute positively to their organization. By fostering a work environment that values both individual growth and job satisfaction, companies can cultivate a motivated and engaged workforce. It is important for organizations to recognize and reward employees for their achievements, while also providing a supportive and encouraging atmosphere that allows for personal and professional development. In doing so, they can create a culture that promotes both individual success and overall organizational success. For example, a company may implement a recognition program where top-performing employees are publicly praised and rewarded with bonuses or promotions. Additionally, offering opportunities for skill development and advancement within the organization can motivate employees to strive for excellence in their work. However, if the recognition program is solely based on favouritism or subjective criteria, it may lead to resentment and demotivation among other employees who feel their hard work is not being acknowledged. Furthermore, if opportunities for skill development are limited or inaccessible to certain employees due to biases or lack of resources, it can hinder overall organizational success and perpetuate inequality within the company.

Impact on Behaviour and Performance

The presence of achievement motivation can lead individuals to strive for excellence in their work, setting high standards for themselves and constantly seeking ways to improve. This drive can result in increased productivity, innovation and job satisfaction. In contrast, employees who lack motivation may become disengaged, leading to decreased productivity, absenteeism and turnover. Therefore, understanding and nurturing achievement motivation can have a positive impact on individual performance and overall organizational success. By recognizing and rewarding employees who demonstrate achievement motivation, organizations can create a culture that values hard work and dedication. This can lead to a more engaged and motivated workforce, ultimately improving overall performance and profitability. Additionally, providing opportunities for growth and development can help individuals cultivate their motivation and drive, leading to long-term success for both the employee and the organization. In conclusion, fostering achievement motivation is essential for creating a high-performing and successful workplace. For example, a company may implement an employee of the month program to recognize and reward outstanding performance, encouraging others to strive for similar achievements. This can create healthy competition and a sense of pride among employees, driving them to excel in their roles and contribute to the organization's success. Additionally, providing opportunities for professional development through training programs and mentorship can also fuel achievement motivation. By investing in their employees' growth and skill development, companies can empower them to reach their full potential and achieve their career goals. Ultimately, a workplace culture that values and promotes achievement motivation can lead to increased productivity, job satisfaction and overall success for the organization. It is clear that nurturing this type of motivation is crucial for building a thriving and high-performing team. For example, a company that offers regular training workshops on new technologies and tools can inspire employees to constantly improve their skills and stay competitive in the industry. Pairing junior employees with experienced mentors can also provide guidance and support in reaching their career aspirations, fostering a culture of continuous learning and growth within the organization.

Strategies for Enhancing Motivation

To enhance achievement motivation, organizations can encourage goal-setting, provide opportunities for skill development and growth and recognize and reward employees for their achievements. Creating a supportive and empowering work environment can also help individuals feel motivated and engaged in their work. Similarly, employee motivation can be enhanced by offering competitive salaries and benefits, providing opportunities for advancement and professional development and fostering a positive organizational culture that values and rewards employee contributions. By investing in training programs and offering mentorship opportunities, organizations can help employees feel valued and supported in their personal and professional growth. Furthermore, fostering open communication and providing regular feedback can help employees understand their progress and areas for improvement, ultimately boosting motivation and productivity. Overall, creating a positive and nurturing work environment is essential for enhancing employee motivation and driving success within the organization.

Why not everyone has Higher Achievement Motivation?

Not everybody can have higher achievement motivation due to a variety of factors, including individual differences, upbringing, experiences and the environment. That's why all employees may not have intrapreneur/entrepreneurship capabilities. Here are some reasons why

1. Personality Traits: Achievement motivation is often associated with certain personality traits, such as conscientiousness, extraversion and openness to experience. Individuals who possess these traits may be more likely to have higher levels of achievement and motivation.

2. Upbringing: The way individuals were raised can greatly impact their levels of achievement motivation. Those who were raised in environments that encouraged goal-setting, perseverance and hard work are more likely to have higher levels of motivation to succeed in their endeavors.

3. Experiences: Past experiences, both positive and negative, can also influence an individual's achievement motivation. Those who have experienced success in the past may be more driven to continue achieving, while those who have faced obstacles or failures may struggle with maintaining high levels of motivation.

4. Environment: The environment in which individuals live and work can also play a significant role in their achievement motivation. A supportive and encouraging work environment can boost motivation, while a toxic or negative environment can hinder it. Creating a positive and nurturing workplace culture is key to fostering high levels of achievement motivation among employees.

2. Upbringing and Environment: The way individuals are raised and the environment in which they grow up can have a significant impact on their motivation levels. Factors such as parental expectations, educational opportunities and socio-economic status can influence the development of achievement motivation.

3. Past Experiences: Previous experiences of success or failure can shape an individual's belief in their ability to achieve goals. Those who have experienced repeated failures may have lower levels of achievement motivation due to a lack of confidence or fear of failure.

4. Goal Orientation: Some individuals may be more focused on learning goals, which involve acquiring new skills and knowledge, rather than performance goals, which involve achieving specific outcomes. This can influence their level of achievement motivation.

5. External Factors: External factors, such as the availability of resources, support from others and the perceived importance of a goal, can also impact achievement motivation. Individuals who perceive a goal as difficult to attain or lacking in significance may have lower levels of motivation.

6. Cultural Differences: Cultural norms and values can play a role in shaping individuals' motivation levels. In some cultures, there may be greater emphasis on individual achievement and success, leading to higher levels of achievement motivation.

While not everyone may have naturally high levels of achievement motivation, it is possible to enhance motivation through various strategies, such as setting specific and challenging goals, providing feedback and support and creating a motivating work environment.

Achievement motivation and employee motivation are crucial factors that influence individual behaviour and performance in the workplace. While achievement motivation drives individuals to excel and succeed, employee motivation encompasses a broader range of factors that influence an individual's willingness to perform effectively in their job. By understanding and nurturing these forms of motivation, organizations can create a work environment that fosters both individual and organizational success. Achievement motivation plays a pivotal role in driving individuals toward entrepreneurship.

Why Achievement Motivation is more in Entrepreneurs?

Let's explore why it is more pronounced among entrepreneurs

1. Goal-Oriented Mindset:

- Entrepreneurs possess a goal-oriented mindset. They set ambitious objectives and strive to achieve high-level goals.

- The desire to create something unique and excel fuels their entrepreneurial journey.

2. Resilience in the Face of Setbacks:

- Entrepreneurship involves navigating challenges, setbacks and uncertainties.

- Achievement motivation acts as a vital fuel, propelling entrepreneurs forward even when faced with obstacles.

3. Competitive Spirit:

- Many entrepreneurs exhibit a competitive spirit. They thrive on achievements, wins and successes.

- The feeling of accomplishment, recognition and praise drives them more than physical or financial rewards.

4. Intrinsic Satisfaction:

- High-achieving entrepreneurs find intrinsic satisfaction in attaining their goals.

- Being at the top of their game, overcoming hurdles and making a difference in their field are powerful motivators.

5. Innovation and Responsibility:

- High-achievers are drawn to innovative activities and responsibility.

- Entrepreneurship provides a platform for them to take charge, create impact and shape their own path.

How to enhance Achievement Motivation in Employees?

In summary, achievement motivation is a driving force for entrepreneurs. It propels them to overcome challenges, innovate and achieve remarkable success in their ventures. Achievement motivation is a powerful force that propels individuals toward their goals. Cultivating this mindset involves intentional actions and strategies. Here are some practical steps to enhance achievement motivation:

1. **Set Specific, Challenging Goals:**

    - Clearly define your objectives. Make them specific and ambitious.

    - Having a target gives you direction and fuels your motivation.

2. **Break Down Large Goals:**

    - Divide big goals into smaller, manageable steps.

- Achieving these smaller milestones provides a sense of progress and keeps you motivated.

3. Track Your Progress:

- Regularly monitor your journey toward your goals.

- Celebrate even the small wins along the way.

4. Embrace a Growth Mindset:

- Believe that abilities can be developed through effort and learning.

- View challenges as opportunities for growth.

5. Build Self-Confidence:

- Recognize your strengths and achievements.

- Confidence fuels motivation and persistence.

6. Learn from Failures:

- Treat setbacks as learning experiences.

- Adapt, adjust and keep moving forward.

7. Surround Yourself with Motivated Individuals:

- Seek out other high-achievers.

- Engage in coffee chats, join community groups, or attend industry events.

Implementing creative employee recognition ideas is vital to talent management in any modern workplace. While competitive pay and benefits attract talent, thoughtful recognition programs boost employee engagement, motivation and loyalty over the long term. Here are 20 practical employee recognition ideas that span various aspects of recognition:

Employee Engagement and recognition Strategies

1. Surprise Days Off:

- When major projects wrap successfully, surprise your teams with an extra 1-2 paid days off. This unexpected time to recharge energizes the team and motivates them for their next project.

2. Team Building Retreats:

- Host quarterly creative retreats that combine engaging activities like cooking classes or sporting events with relationship-building workshops. Bonding while having fun will motivate your teams.

3. Celebration Events for Team Achievements:

- Organize team celebrations for hitting milestones, completing projects, or achieving goals. It could be a themed party, lunch, or dinner outing.

4. Personalized Thank-You Notes:

- Write heartfelt thank-you note to individual employees, highlighting their specific contributions. Personalization shows genuine appreciation.

5. Peer-to-Peer Recognition Programs:

- Encourage colleagues to recognize each other's achievements. Implement a system where employees can nominate their peers for outstanding work.

6. Wall of Fame or Recognition Board:

- Create a physical or virtual space where you display photos and achievements of outstanding employees. Regularly update it to keep the motivation alive.

7. Customized Awards:

- Design unique awards or trophies for exceptional performance. Consider fun categories like "Innovation Guru" or "Customer Whisperer."

8. Spotlight in Company Newsletter or Website:

- Acknowledge individual achievements at team meetings or in the company newsletter. Spotlight employees' stories or accomplishments on the company website or through social media shoutouts.

9. Employee Appreciation Days:

- Designate specific days or weeks to celebrate and appreciate employees' contributions. Plan various activities, such as team-building games, themed dress-up days, contests and surprise treats to make these days extra special.

10. Virtual High-Fives or Applause:

- Use collaboration tools or communication channels to send virtual high-fives or applause emojis when someone achieves a milestone.

11. Customized Desk Decorations:

- Surprise employees by decorating their desks with balloons, streamers, or personalized banners when they achieve something significant.

12. Lunch with Leadership:

- Invite high-performing employees to have lunch with senior leaders. It's an excellent opportunity for informal conversations and recognition.

13. Employee of the Month/Quarter:

- Recognize outstanding employees publicly by featuring them as the employee of the month or quarter. Include their photo and a brief write-up.

14. Learning and Development Opportunities:

- Offer courses, workshops, or certifications related to employees' interests or career growth. Recognize their commitment to learning.

15. Customized Gifts or Swag Bags:

- Surprise employees with personalized gifts, such as branded merchandise, tech gadgets, or wellness items.

16. Wall of Quotes or Inspirational Messages:

- Create a wall with motivational quotes or messages contributed by employees. It fosters a positive environment.

17. Random Acts of Kindness:

- Encourage employees to perform random acts of kindness for their colleagues. Recognize those who go the extra mile.

18. Flexible Work Arrangements:

- Recognize exceptional performance by offering flexible work hours, remote work options, or compressed workweeks.

19. Public Shoutouts in Meetings:

- During team meetings, publicly acknowledge employees' achievements and express gratitude for their hard work.

20. Create a Recognition Committee:

- Form a committee responsible for planning and executing creative recognition initiatives. Involve employees from different departments.

The key to effective recognition is authenticity and consistency. Tailor these ideas to your company culture and the preferences of your employees. Employee motivation refers to the energization and direction of behaviour in the workplace. It encompasses both intrinsic (internal) and extrinsic (external) factors that encourage employee engagement, commitment and satisfaction. Essentially, it's what drives employees to act and perform their tasks effectively.

On the other hand, achievement motivation specifically focuses on the need for success or the attainment of excellence. It examines the driving forces behind striving toward competence (success) and away from incompetence (failure). Individuals with high achievement motivation are dedicated to developing and demonstrating higher abilities. This concept is one of the components in McClelland's Human Motivation Theory, proposed by social psychologist David McClelland, who studied workplace motivation.

In summary:

- Employee motivation encompasses a broader range of factors that influence overall engagement and satisfaction.

- Achievement motivation specifically relates to the desire for success and excellence in specific tasks or goals.

Achievement motivation significantly influences work performance in various ways. Here are some examples:

1. Increased Productivity:

- Employees with high achievement motivation tend to be more productive. They set challenging goals, work diligently and strive for excellence.

- Their desire to achieve drives them to put in extra effort, resulting in higher output.

2. Quality Work Output:

- Individuals with achievement motivation focus on delivering high-quality work.

- They pay attention to details, seek continuous improvement and take pride in their accomplishments.

3. Innovation and Problem-Solving:

- Achievement-motivated employees actively seek innovative solutions.

- They tackle challenges creatively, explore new approaches and contribute fresh ideas.

4. Goal Attainment:

- These individuals are persistent in pursuing their objectives.

- They set clear targets, monitor progress and adjust strategies to achieve success.

5. Adaptability and Resilience:

- High achievers handle setbacks effectively.

- They learn from failures, adapt to changing circumstances and maintain a positive attitude.

6. Collaboration and Teamwork:

- Achievement motivation encourages collaboration.

- These employees willingly collaborate with colleagues to achieve collective goals.

7. Career Advancement:

- Individuals with strong achievement motivation actively seek growth opportunities.

- They take on challenging projects, acquire new skills and position themselves for promotions.

8. Employee Retention:

- Motivated employees are more likely to stay with the organization.

- Their sense of accomplishment and alignment with organizational goals fosters loyalty.

9. Positive Organizational Culture:

- A team of achievement-motivated individuals contributes to a positive work environment.

- Their enthusiasm and commitment inspire others.

10. Customer Satisfaction:

- High achievers go the extra mile to meet customer needs.

- Their dedication to excellence enhances customer experiences.

Achievement motivation positively impacts work performance by driving productivity, quality, innovation and collaboration. Organizations benefit from fostering this mindset among employees. Remember, achievement motivation is not just about reaching the destination—it's about enjoying the journey and continually striving for improvement. When employees embody achievement motivation, they bring a sense of drive and purpose to their work. This not only leads to personal success but also contributes to a positive work environment. Their enthusiasm and commitment inspire others to do their best and work towards common goals. Ultimately, this dedication to excellence enhances customer experiences and increases overall satisfaction. By cultivating a culture of achievement motivation, organizations can see improved performance and success across the board.

Risk Taking Appetite

Chapter-7

Chapter-7: Risk Taking Appetite

In the context of developing nations, the interplay between working hours and productivity is a critical consideration. Both factors significantly impact economic growth, individual well-being and overall societal progress. "Not taking risks itself is a big risk": Embracing the Power of Risk-Taking for Personal Growth and Success Life is filled with opportunities, challenges and uncertainties.

At times, the fear of failure or the comfort of the familiar may dissuade us from taking risks. However, it is essential to recognize that not taking risks itself is a significant risk. Stagnation missed opportunities and a lack of personal growth can result from avoiding risk-taking. Embracing calculated risks can lead to transformative experiences, enhanced self-confidence and the potential for great rewards.

This chapter delves into the reasons why not taking risks can be a substantial risk and explores how calculated risk-taking can be a catalyst for personal growth and success. By stepping out of our comfort zones and taking calculated risks, we open ourselves up to new possibilities and experiences that can shape us into better versions of ourselves. These risks may involve starting a new business venture, pursuing a passion project, or even engaging in a new relationship. While there is always the possibility of failure or disappointment, the potential for growth and success far outweighs the comfort and security of remaining stagnant. Ultimately, it is through taking risks that we truly discover our potential and unlock the doors to personal growth and success.

What makes people not to take risks?

1. Missed Opportunities: Not taking risks can lead to missed opportunities in both personal and professional realms. Opportunities for career advancement, starting a business, forming new relationships, or pursuing a passion project may pass by if one remains complacent and unwilling to take a leap of faith. By playing it safe, individuals may find themselves stuck in unfulfilling routines with a lingering sense of "what if?" It is crucial to recognize that life's greatest rewards often come with a certain degree of uncertainty and seizing opportunities requires a willingness to take risks.

Taking risks can be intimidating, as it involves stepping out of one's comfort zone and facing the unknown. However, it is important to remember that growth and personal development often occur outside of our comfort zones. Embracing uncertainty and taking calculated risks can lead to incredible personal and professional growth, opening doors to new experiences and possibilities that may have otherwise been missed. For example, a person who is hesitant to start their own business due to the uncertainty of the market and potential failure may miss out on the opportunity to become a successful entrepreneur. However, if they are willing to take the risk and embrace the uncertainty, they may discover innovative solutions and create a thriving business that brings them fulfilment and financial success.

2. Limited Personal Growth: Growth and self-discovery often come through stepping out of one's comfort zone. By avoiding risks, individuals may deny themselves valuable learning experiences that push them to develop new skills and perspectives. Taking risks can challenge preconceived notions and broaden horizons, fostering personal growth and resilience. Failure, which is often feared when taking risks, is also an opportunity for learning and improvement. Each failure brings valuable lessons that can be instrumental in future successes.

By embracing failure and viewing it as a stepping stone towards success, individuals can develop a growth mindset and become more adaptable to change. Additionally, taking risks can also lead to unexpected opportunities and open doors that may not have been possible otherwise. For example, a young entrepreneur who takes a risk and starts their own business may face initial failure and setbacks. However, by learning from their mistakes and making the necessary adjustments, they can use these experiences to refine their business strategies and ultimately achieve success. Additionally, this entrepreneur may encounter unexpected opportunities, such as meeting influential mentors or gaining valuable industry connections that propel their business to new heights.

3. Regret and "What If" Scenarios: Regret can weigh heavily on those who allow fear to prevent them from taking risks. The persistent question "What if I had tried?" can haunt individuals throughout their lives. The discomfort of regret can be more profound than the discomfort of a temporary setback resulting from a risk taken.

By embracing risk-taking, individuals can eliminate the uncertainty of missed opportunities and the nagging feeling of wondering what could have been. By embracing risk-taking, individuals can experience personal growth and self-discovery. Stepping out of one's comfort zone and taking risks can lead to new experiences, skills and perspectives that can enhance one's life. Additionally, embracing risk-taking can build resilience and confidence as individuals learn to overcome challenges and navigate uncertainty. Ultimately, by choosing to take risks, individuals empower themselves to live a life without regrets, knowing that they have given their best and seized every opportunity that comes their way.

For example, someone who has always been afraid of public speaking may decide to join a Toastmasters club in order to overcome their fear and improve their communication skills. By stepping out of their comfort zone and taking the risk of speaking in front of others, they not only gain valuable speaking skills but also develop confidence and resilience as they face their fear head-on. This newfound ability to take risks and embrace challenges can then extend beyond public speaking, allowing them to tackle other areas of personal and professional growth with a

4. Lack of Adaptability: Life is dynamic and the ability to adapt to change is crucial. Avoiding risk-taking can lead to a reluctance to embrace change and adapt to new circumstances. In contrast, taking calculated risks enhances adaptability and fosters a mindset of resilience and resourcefulness. Those who regularly take risks become more adept at navigating uncertainty and are better equipped to handle unexpected challenges. By actively seeking out new experiences and challenges, individuals can develop a greater sense of adaptability. This can involve stepping outside of one's comfort zone, trying new things and being open to different perspectives. Embracing risk-taking as a means of personal and professional growth can ultimately lead to increased adaptability in all aspects of life.

For example, someone who regularly takes risks may decide to start their own business. This venture involves navigating the uncertainties of the market, making strategic decisions and handling unexpected challenges such as changing customer demands or economic downturns. Through this experience, they develop greater adaptability to handle uncertainty and are better equipped to handle future challenges in their personal and professional lives.

5. Stagnation and Mediocrity: Comfort zones can become breeding grounds for mediocrity and stagnation. When individuals resist stepping beyond the familiar, they limit their potential for growth and success. Taking risks propels individuals towards new challenges and possibilities, setting the stage for exceptional achievements and breakthroughs. Without the willingness to take risks, individuals may become complacent and settle for mediocrity, robbing themselves of the opportunity to reach their full potential. By embracing discomfort and pushing the boundaries of their comfort zones, individuals expose themselves to new perspectives and experiences. This not only fosters personal growth but also cultivates resilience and adaptability, qualities that are crucial in an ever-changing world.

For example, an entrepreneur who is afraid of failure may never take the risk of starting their own business. By staying within their comfort zone, they miss out on the opportunity to create a successful company and make a significant impact in their industry. On the other hand, an entrepreneur who embraces discomfort and takes calculated risks may experience failures along the way but ultimately learn valuable lessons that lead to exceptional achievements and breakthrough innovations.

6. **Building Resilience:** Calculated risk-taking builds resilience and fosters a positive attitude towards failure. Resilience is the ability to bounce back from setbacks and risk-taking provides ample opportunities for developing this invaluable trait. Embracing risk means accepting that setbacks and failures are part of the journey towards success. Learning to persevere in the face of adversity is a crucial skill for overcoming obstacles and achieving long-term goals.

Not taking risks itself is a big risk

"Not taking risks itself is a big risk" is an adage that carries profound truth.

Avoiding risk-taking may seem comfortable and secure, but it comes with a high cost: missed opportunities, limited personal growth, regret and the stagnation of potential. Embracing calculated risks opens doors to transformative experiences, personal growth and the potential for outstanding success. Risks may bring temporary setbacks, but the rewards can be life-changing, leading to newfound confidence, adaptability and resilience. Ultimately, taking risks propels individuals towards fulfilling their dreams, reaching their full potential and living a life of purpose and accomplishment. By recognizing and embracing the power of risk-taking, individuals can break free from the shackles of complacency and discover the vast possibilities that await beyond their comfort zones. Stepping outside of one's comfort zone allows individuals to explore new opportunities and learn valuable lessons that can contribute to personal growth and development.

It is through taking risks that individuals can push their limits, overcome obstacles and unlock their true potential. By embracing risk-taking as a necessary part of personal and professional growth, individuals can create a life filled with excitement, fulfilment and meaningful experiences. Some individuals may argue that stepping outside of one's comfort zone can also lead to failure, disappointment and unnecessary stress, ultimately hindering personal growth and development.

SMART THEORY FOR
EMPLOYEE EVALUATIONS
CHAPTER-8
Ready for a 1-on-1?
WORLD'S
BEST
BOSS
it's time for performance review!
@dibyenduchoudhury

Chapter 8: SMART Theory for Employee Evaluations

In many instances, we find ourselves in situations within a majority of poorly managed organizations where the evaluation system is entirely subjective. In such cases, proximity to superiors, influence, relationships and various other factors play a crucial role in determining the level of appreciation reflected in compensation and salary hikes. Interestingly, this phenomenon is not exclusive to small and medium-sized enterprises (SMEs); I've observed it occurring even in large public sector undertakings (PSUs) in India, despite the country's emphasis on being system-driven.

However, where there is a system, there are bound to be bugs. These bugs need to be identified and fixed. It reminds me of a popular saying by **Edsger Dijkstra** "If debugging is the process of removing software bugs, then programming must be the process of putting them in."

The SMART goals are easy to remember, objective and goal oriented. It is essential for organizations to continuously review their systems and processes to ensure that they are functioning effectively and efficiently. Implementing regular checks and audits can help in identifying and resolving any issues that may arise. By following the principles of SMART goals - specific, measurable, achievable, relevant and time-bound - companies can ensure that they are on the right track towards success and growth. Ultimately, it is important for businesses to adapt and evolve in order to stay competitive in today's dynamic and fast-paced market.

Now, let's delve into the concept of SMART goals:

- **Specific (S):** Goals should be well-defined and precise. They should answer questions like "What?" and "Why?"

- **Measurable (M):** Goals should be quantifiable, allowing progress to be tracked and evaluated.

- **Achievable (A):** Goals should be realistic and attainable within the given resources and constraints.

- **Relevant (R):** Goals should align with the overall objectives of the organization or individual.

- **Time-Bound (T):** Goals should have a specific timeframe for completion.

By adhering to the SMART framework, organizations and individuals can create effective and well-defined goals that lead to success.

1. Specific (S):

- Goals should be clearly defined and focused.

- Answer questions like: What needs to be accomplished? Who is responsible? What steps are required?

2. Measurable (M):

- Goals should be quantifiable so that progress can be tracked.

- Set specific metrics or criteria to measure success.

3. Achievable (A):

- Goals should be realistic and attainable.

- Consider available resources, skills and constraints.

4. Relevant (R):

- Goals should be aligned with your overall objectives.

- Ensure they contribute to your larger purpose.

5. Time-Bound (T):

- Goals should have a specific timeframe for completion.

- Set deadlines to create a sense of urgency.

For example, a SMART goal might be: "Increase monthly users of our mobile app by 20% within the next quarter by optimizing our app-store listing and running targeted social media campaigns."

By following the SMART framework, individuals and teams can set clear, achievable objectives and stay on track toward success.

S.M.A.R.T

Employee motivation is crucial for organizational success. While some individuals naturally exhibit high achievement motivation, others may need encouragement. Here are strategies to foster motivation among employees:

1. Set clear Goals:

- Specific, challenging goals provide direction and purpose.

- Collaboratively set targets and celebrate achievements when they are accomplished.

2. Provide Regular Feedback and Coaching:

- Constructive feedback helps employees understand their progress.

- Regular coaching sessions enhance performance and motivation.

3.   Encourage   Autonomy   and Empowerment:

- Allow employees to make decisions and take ownership of their work.

- Autonomy fosters a sense of responsibility and achievement.

4. Create a Culture of Appreciation:

- Recognize and reward achievements.

- Appreciation can be verbal, through awards, or even small gestures.

5. Invest in Training and Development:

- Job enrichment and advancement opportunities enhance engagement.

- Provide specific training to improve job performance.

6. Promote a Positive Workplace Culture:

- A supportive environment encourages motivation.

- Foster collaboration, respect and camaraderie.

7. Link Individual Goals to Organizational Objectives:

- Show employees how their work contributes to the bigger picture.

- Align personal achievements with company success.

8. Provide Competitive Compensation and Benefits:

- Fair pay and benefits motivate employees.

- Incentives and bonuses can boost achievement motivation.

Remember that motivation is not a one-size-fits-all approach. Tailor strategies to individual needs and preferences. Recognizing and rewarding employees based on their unique strengths and contributions can also increase motivation and job satisfaction. Additionally, offering opportunities for professional development and growth can further incentivize employees to perform at their best. By creating a positive and supportive work environment, aligning individual goals with organizational objectives and providing competitive compensation and benefits, employers can cultivate a motivated and engaged workforce that drives company success.

How to enhance Employee Motivation?

Here are examples of how these strategies can enhance motivation:

1. Setting Specific and Challenging Goals:

- Example: In a sales team, setting specific sales targets for each member for the quarter can motivate them to strive harder to achieve those targets. These goals should be challenging yet attainable, pushing individuals to stretch their abilities.

2. Providing Feedback and Support:

- Example: In an educational setting, providing students with constructive feedback on their assignments can motivate them to improve. Positive feedback can reinforce good performance, while constructive criticism can guide them on areas for improvement.

3. Creating a Motivating Work Environment:

- Example: A company can create a motivating work environment by fostering a culture of collaboration and recognition. For instance, implementing an "Employee of the Month" program can motivate employees to perform better, knowing that their efforts will be recognized and rewarded.

Overall, these strategies focus on creating a supportive and empowering environment that encourages individuals to take ownership of their goals, seek continuous improvement and feel motivated to perform at their best.

There are disparities between employers and employees. Regardless of the linguistic differences, employees rarely adopt an employer attitude due to their risk-taking tendencies. Employers can assist bridge the gap between themselves and their employees by cultivating an open communication and cooperation culture.

Encourage feedback, provide chances for growth and development and recognize each individual's unique skills and contributions can all assist to foster a sense of unity and shared purpose inside the business. Employees who feel appreciated and respected are more likely to embrace tasks and responsibilities with a sense of ownership and commitment. Finally, by creating a happy and inclusive work atmosphere, companies may motivate their employees to strive for excellence and contribute to the company's overall success.

This positive work environment can also lead to increased employee engagement, productivity and retention rates. Additionally, by promoting a culture of transparency and trust, organizations can build strong relationships with their employees, leading to improved communication, collaboration and problem-solving abilities. Ultimately, by prioritizing the well-being and satisfaction of their workforce, companies can create a thriving and sustainable business that attracts top talent and drives long-term success.

Differences between an entrepreneur and an intrapreneur

Now let's explore the basic differences between an entrepreneur and an intrapreneur:

1. Entrepreneur:

Definition: An entrepreneur is an individual who conceives of a new business venture and takes significant risks to establish and operate that business. Entrepreneurs often create startups from scratch.

- **Independence:** Entrepreneurs operate independently and are responsible for the entire business.

- **Risk:** They bear the full risk associated with the success or failure of their venture.

- **Resource Utilization:** Entrepreneurs use their own resources (such as capital, skills and networks) to build the business.

- **Goal:** Their primary goal is to create a leading position in the market by introducing innovative products, services, or business models.

2. Intrapreneur:

- **Definition:** An intrapreneur, on the other hand, is an employee within an existing organization who promotes innovation and entrepreneurial behaviour within the company.

- **Role:** Intrapreneurs work within the boundaries of the organization, leveraging its resources and infrastructure.

- **Responsibility:** They are tasked with undertaking innovations in products, services, processes, or systems.

- **Risk:** Unlike entrepreneurs, intrapreneurs do not bear the full risk; instead, the company absorbs it.

- **Objective:** Their primary objective is to renew and transform existing organizational systems, culture and practices.

While both entrepreneurs and intrapreneurs exhibit qualities like creativity and insight, the key difference lies in their context and scope. Entrepreneurs create new ventures independently, while intrapreneurs drive innovation within established organizations.

Narayana Murthy, the founder of Infosys, believes that if India wants to make significant progress, then the Indian youth will have to step up productivity and work hard.

After examining this chapter, we can immediately appreciate the significant differences between the roles and responsibilities of an entrepreneur and an intrapreneur. An entrepreneur takes on the full risks associated with their venture, bearing the entire burden of ensuring the business's success. This includes the pressure of managing cash flow, covering operational expenses and ultimately ensuring that bills are paid at the end of each month. Such immense responsibility drives entrepreneurs to put in extended hours, maximizing their use of available resources and striving diligently to achieve their targets. The success or failure of the business rests squarely on their shoulders, motivating them to relentlessly push their limits and innovate continuously.

In contrast, an intrapreneur operates within the framework of an existing organization, assuming only a partial risk of the enterprise. While they are responsible for driving innovation and spearheading new projects, the ultimate financial risk does not fall entirely on their shoulders. The parent organization absorbs most of the financial pressures and uncertainties, providing a safety net that allows intrapreneurs to focus more on creative processes and strategic development without the imminent fear of financial failure.

This fundamental difference in risk assumption creates a distinct dynamic between entrepreneurs and intrapreneurs. Entrepreneurs adopt a more hands-on, intensive approach because they want to ensure the survival and growth of their business. They often juggle multiple roles, make critical decisions under pressure and face the consequences of their choices directly. Their personal and financial well-being is intricately tied to the success of their venture, fostering a high-stakes environment that demands resilience, dedication and an unwavering commitment to their vision.

On the other hand, intrapreneurs benefit from the stability and resources provided by their organizations. Although they are still responsible for the success of their initiatives, the organization's wider support structure reduces the risk. This allows intrapreneurs to experiment, take calculated risks and innovate without the looming threat of personal financial loss. The organizational backing provides a buffer that encourages creativity and strategic thinking, enabling intrapreneurs to contribute significantly to the company's growth while maintaining a balanced approach to risk and reward.

The distinction between entrepreneurs and intrapreneurs lies in the level of risk assumed and the consequent pressures faced. Entrepreneurs, bearing the full brunt of their venture's risks, are driven to work tirelessly to ensure success. Intrapreneurs, with their partial risk assumption, operate within a more secure environment that fosters innovation and creativity without the immediate financial pressures.

This difference fundamentally shapes their approaches, motivations and contributions to the business landscape. Infact, he suggests that the younger generation should be prepared to work 70 hours a week because India is just standing at the juncture to become the developed Nation with enormous opportunities in the coming time The government has already established an entrepreneur-friendly environment which technically we call "Entrepreneurial Ecosystem."

Insights From Shri Narayan Murthy for the young Hustlers

Murthy suggested with his insights to the youngsters in the debut episode of "The Record," a video series by 3one4 Capital. He emphasizes the need for Indian youth to pick the right habits from the West and avoid undesirable ones. According to him, our youth sometimes adopt habits that are not conducive to the country's growth. By working diligently and putting in long hours, he hopes they can contribute to India's development.

 Murthy draws inspiration from countries like China, which have made significant economic progress over the last few decades. He encourages Indian leaders to learn from successful nations and implement effective policy decisions. Bureaucratic efficiency is another area he advocates for, as reducing delays in decision-making can enhance India's global competitiveness. In summary, Narayana Murthy's call for longer work hours is rooted in the belief that increased productivity and hard work are essential for India's advancement on the world stage and India is right now ready for harnessing all the young talents with innovative ideas and become its time for awakening for the sleeping giant.

Narayana Murthy draws inspiration from the remarkable economic progress achieved by countries like China over the past few decades. He highlights the transformative journey of such nations, which have implemented strategic policy decisions to propel their economies forward. Murthy encourages Indian leaders to study these successful models and adapt their strategies to suit India's unique context. He believes that by learning from these global examples, India can implement effective policies that drive economic growth and development.

Murthy also emphasizes the need for bureaucratic efficiency, advocating for streamlined processes and reduced delays in decision-making. He argues that enhancing bureaucratic efficiency is crucial for improving India's global competitiveness. By cutting down on red tape and accelerating administrative procedures, India can create a more conducive environment for business and innovation.

In addition to policy and bureaucratic reforms, Murthy calls for a cultural shift towards increased productivity and hard work. He believes that longer work hours, coupled with a strong work ethic, are vital for India's advancement on the global stage. According to Murthy, this dedication to productivity will harness the full potential of India's vast pool of young talent and innovative minds.

Murthy's vision for India is one of a "sleeping giant" ready to awaken. With its youthful population and burgeoning entrepreneurial spirit, India stands at the cusp of a significant transformation. By fostering an environment that encourages innovation, supports hard work and implements efficient policies, India can rise to its full potential and achieve unprecedented economic growth.

Narayana Murthy's call to action encompasses learning from global success stories, improving bureaucratic efficiency and cultivating a culture of productivity and hard work. He believes that these elements are essential for India's progress and that the nation is primed to harness its young talent and innovative ideas. This, he asserts, is India's moment to awaken and emerge as a formidable force on the world stage.

CHAPTER-9

ENHANCING PATRIOTISM: A CRUCIAL ELEMENT FOR NATIONAL PROGRESS

Chapter 9: Enhancing Patriotism: A Crucial Element for National Progress

Patriotism is an emotion that can be nurtured in various ways. One of the most effective ways to enhance patriotism is through education. By teaching citizens about the history and values of their country, they can develop a deeper appreciation for their nation. Additionally, fostering a sense of unity and pride in one's country through community events and celebrations can also help to strengthen patriotism. Ultimately, a strong sense of patriotism is crucial for national progress, as it motivates individuals to work towards the common good and strive for the betterment of their country.

This can be seen in times of crisis, where patriotic citizens come together to support and protect their nation. Furthermore, promoting patriotism can also lead to increased civic engagement and a sense of responsibility towards one's community and fellow citizens. In this way, patriotism not only benefits the individual but also society as a whole, creating a more cohesive and prosperous nation. By instilling a sense of pride and loyalty in its citizens, a country can build a strong foundation for success and progress.

How to Improve Patriotism?

Here are some factors that can help improve patriotism:

1. Education: Education can play a crucial role in fostering patriotism by teaching citizens about their country's history, culture and values. It can also help promote critical thinking and civic engagement, which are essential for a healthy democracy.

2. National symbols and traditions: National symbols such as the flag, national anthem and national holidays can help foster a sense of pride and unity among citizens. Celebrating national holidays and participating in national events can also help promote a sense of community and shared identity.

3. Service to the nation: Serving the nation through military service, public service, or volunteering can help instil a sense of duty and responsibility among citizens. It can also help promote a sense of shared sacrifice and commitment to the common good.

4. Promoting diversity and inclusion: Promoting diversity and inclusion can help create a sense of belonging among citizens from different backgrounds and cultures. It can also help promote a sense of unity and shared values among citizens.

5. Encouraging civic engagement: Encouraging civic engagement through voting, community involvement and political participation can help promote a sense of responsibility and ownership among citizens. It can also help promote a sense of empowerment and agency among citizens.

These are just some of the factors that can help improve patriotism. However, it's important to note that patriotism should be anchored in shared values such as respect for human rights, democracy and the rule of law. Education can play a crucial role in fostering patriotism by teaching citizens about their country's history, culture and values Patriotism should be anchored in shared values such as respect for human rights, democracy and the rule of law.

Education can also help promote critical thinking and civic engagement, which are essential for a healthy democracy. National symbols such as the flag, national anthem and national holidays can help foster a sense of pride and unity among citizens.

Serving the nation through military service, public service, or volunteering can help instil a sense of duty and responsibility among citizens. It can also help promote a sense of shared sacrifice and commitment to the common good.

Promoting diversity and inclusion can help create a sense of belonging among citizens from different backgrounds and cultures. It can also help promote a sense of unity and shared values among citizens. Encouraging civic engagement through voting, community involvement and political participation can help promote a sense of responsibility and ownership among citizens. It can also help promote a sense of empowerment and agency among citizens.

Patriotism is an emotion that can be nurtured in various ways. While poverty can be a significant challenge for any nation, it's important to note that patriotism can play a crucial role in promoting social harmony, unity and shared values among citizens. Patriotism can inspire individuals to work together for the betterment of their country, take pride in their country's achievements and contribute to its continued success.

However, it's important to note that patriotism should not be used as a tool to ignore or downplay the challenges faced by the citizens of a country. Poverty, inequality and social injustice are significant issues that need to be addressed for any nation to thrive. Therefore, it's essential to promote a sense of patriotism anchored in shared values such as respect for human rights, democracy and the rule of law, which can help create a more inclusive and equitable society and instil the trust and faith of the common people in the Governance.

In conclusion, while poverty can be a significant challenge for any nation, patriotism can play a crucial role in promoting social harmony, unity and shared values among citizens. However, it's important to promote a sense of patriotism anchored in shared values such as respect for human rights, democracy and the rule of law, which can help create a more inclusive and equitable society.

Patriotism, the deep sense of love and devotion to one's country, plays an indispensable role in the development and progress of a nation. It fosters unity, motivates citizens to contribute positively and underpins national resilience. Without a robust sense of patriotism, efforts towards economic, social and cultural advancements may falter. This essay delves into the significance of patriotism, its manifestations and the ways in which it can be enhanced to drive national progress.

The Importance of Patriotism

Unity and National Identity

Patriotism fosters a shared sense of identity and belonging among citizens. It unites people across diverse backgrounds, ethnicities and religions, creating a cohesive national identity. This unity is crucial for maintaining social harmony and stability. For instance, India's rich tapestry of cultures and languages is bound together by a shared sense of patriotism, despite the country's diversity.

Motivation for Civic Participation

A strong sense of patriotism motivates citizens to participate actively in civic duties, such as voting, community service and public discourse. This engagement is vital for a functioning democracy and for ensuring that the government remains accountable to its people. In the United States, for example, patriotic sentiments have historically driven significant movements for civil rights and social justice, reflecting citizens' commitment to national values. The country prioritizes democracy and civil rights and has the authority to imp itch former president and bring him to justice in criminal courts. This level of accountability is a pillar of democracy, setting a strong example for other countries around the world. Citizens can influence their country's future and work toward a more just and equitable society by actively participating in civic obligations and holding leaders accountable. This shared dedication to democracy and civil rights enhances a nation's foundation and builds solidarity among its citizens.

Economic Development

Patriotism can drive economic development by encouraging citizens to support domestic industries and products. A patriotic populace is more likely to buy locally made goods, invest in national enterprises and support government initiatives aimed at economic growth. For example, the "Make in India" campaign leverages patriotic sentiments to boost domestic manufacturing and reduce dependency on imports.

National Resilience

Patriotism strengthens national resilience by fostering a collective will to overcome challenges, whether they be economic crises, natural disasters, or external threats. During times of crisis, patriotic feelings can galvanize citizens to work together, support each other and contribute to recovery efforts. The resilience of the Japanese people in the aftermath of the 2011 tsunami and nuclear disaster is a testament to the power of patriotism in the face of adversity.

Manifestations of Patriotism

Patriotism manifests in various forms, each contributing to the overall well-being and progress of a nation. These manifestations include:

National Service

Volunteering for national service, such as military duty or community projects, is a direct expression of patriotism. Citizens who serve their country demonstrate a willingness to put national interests above personal gain. In countries like Israel, mandatory military service fosters a strong sense of duty and patriotism among young citizens.

Cultural Preservation

Patriotism often involves preserving and promoting a nation's cultural heritage. This includes celebrating national holidays, promoting traditional arts and crafts and safeguarding historical sites. In India, festivals like Independence Day and Republic Day are celebrated with great fervour, reinforcing national pride and cultural identity.

Political Engagement

Active political engagement, including voting, participating in political debates and holding public office, is a key expression of patriotism. Citizens who engage in the political process demonstrate their commitment to shaping the future of their country. The high voter turnout in the recent general elections in India reflects the citizens' patriotic duty to participate in the democratic process.

Economic Patriotism

Supporting domestic industries and products is a practical way of expressing patriotism. This involves choosing locally made goods, investing in national enterprises and supporting government economic initiatives. Campaigns like "Vocal for Local" in India aim to boost domestic consumption and reduce reliance on foreign products.

Enhancing Patriotism

Given the crucial role of patriotism in national progress, it is essential to actively cultivate and enhance patriotic sentiments among citizens. This can be done through education, promoting national symbols and values and encouraging active engagement in community service and civic activities. By fostering a sense of pride and loyalty towards their country, citizens are more likely to contribute positively to its development and growth. Ultimately, a strong sense of patriotism can lead to a more united and prosperous nation. This can be achieved through various strategies:

Public Celebrations and Rituals

Public celebrations and rituals, such as Independence Day, Republic Dayan other national holidays, play a significant role in enhancing patriotism. These events bring citizens together to celebrate their shared heritage and achievements. They also provide opportunities to honour national heroes and reflect on the country's progress. For example, the annual Republic Day parade in India showcases the nation's cultural diversity and military strength, instilling pride among citizens.

Media and Communication

The media has a powerful influence on public sentiment and can be instrumental in promoting patriotism. Positive stories about national achievements, progress and inspiring individuals can foster a sense of pride and unity. Governments can collaborate with media outlets to highlight stories of national significance and promote patriotic values. The Indian film industry, Bollywood, often produces films that celebrate national heroes and historical events, reinforcing patriotic sentiments among audiences.

Community Engagement

Community engagement initiatives, such as volunteering and social service, can foster a sense of responsibility and pride among citizens. Encouraging individuals to participate in community projects, environmental conservation and social welfare activities can strengthen their connection to the nation. Programs like the National Service Scheme (NSS) in India involve students in community service, promoting a sense of civic duty and patriotism.

Role of Leaders

National leaders play a crucial role in shaping and promoting patriotic sentiments. By exemplifying patriotism in their actions and rhetoric, leaders can inspire citizens to adopt similar values. Leaders who demonstrate integrity, dedication and a commitment to national interests can galvanize public support and foster a strong sense of patriotism. Mahatma Gandhi, India's preeminent leader during the independence movement, inspired millions with his unwavering commitment to the nation.

Case Studies and Global Examples

United States: Patriotism in Education and Media

In the United States, patriotism is deeply ingrained in the education system and media. Programs like "We the People" promote civic education, teaching students about the Constitution, democratic values and national history. Additionally, American media often highlights stories of national achievements, military service and community heroes, fostering a strong sense of national pride. The celebration of Independence Day on July 4th, with fireworks, parades and patriotic displays, exemplifies the country's commitment to promoting patriotism.

Japan: Cultural Preservation and National Resilience

Japan's sense of patriotism is closely tied to cultural preservation and national resilience. The country places a strong emphasis on preserving traditional arts, crafts and customs, which are seen as integral to national identity. Public holidays like National Foundation Day and Emperor's Birthday are celebrated with reverence, reinforcing a sense of unity and pride. The resilience and teamwork of Japan's people, driven by a strong sense of patriotism, were on full display in their response to the tsunami and nuclear disaster in 2011.

Israel: National Service and Civic Duty

In Israel, mandatory military service for both men and women fosters a strong sense of duty and patriotism among citizens. This national service instils values of responsibility, commitment and sacrifice for the country. Additionally, Israel celebrates national holidays like Independence Day with great fervour, reinforcing national unity and pride. The country's emphasis on innovation and resilience in the face of challenges further strengthens patriotic sentiments among its citizens.

India: Public Celebrations and Community Engagement

India's sense of patriotism is vividly expressed through public celebrations and community engagement. National holidays like Independence Day and Republic Day are marked by grand parades, cultural performances and patriotic speeches, bringing citizens together to celebrate their shared heritage. Community engagement initiatives, such as the Swachh Bharat Abhiyan (Clean India Mission), encourage citizens to participate in nation-building activities, fostering a sense of responsibility and pride.

Challenges to Enhancing Patriotism

While fostering patriotism is crucial, there are several challenges that need to be addressed:

Diversity and Regionalism

In countries with diverse populations, regional identities and loyalties can sometimes overshadow national identity. Balancing these regional affiliations with a sense of national unity is a complex but essential task. In India, regionalism can sometimes pose challenges to national unity, requiring efforts to promote inclusivity and a shared national identity.

Political Polarization

Political polarization can erode patriotic sentiments by creating divisions within society. When political discourse becomes excessively partisan, it can undermine the collective sense of national identity. Efforts to foster patriotism must navigate these political divides and emphasize common values and goals.

Economic Disparities

Economic inequalities can lead to disillusionment and a lack of national pride among disadvantaged populations. Addressing these disparities through inclusive policies and equitable development is essential to foster a sense of belonging and patriotism. Ensuring that all citizens benefit from national progress is crucial for maintaining patriotic sentiments.

Globalization

Globalization can sometimes dilute national identities by promoting a more cosmopolitan worldview. While embracing global interconnectedness, it is important to preserve and promote national heritage and values. Balancing global engagement with the preservation of national identity requires a nuanced approach.

Strategies to Overcome Challenges

Inclusive Policies

Implementing inclusive policies that address regional disparities, economic inequalities and social injustices can strengthen national unity and patriotism. Ensuring that all citizens, regardless of their background, feel valued and included in the national narrative is essential.

Bipartisan Initiatives

Promoting bipartisan initiatives that emphasize national goals and values can help bridge political divides and foster a sense of unity. National service programs, community projects and public celebrations can serve as platforms for bipartisan collaboration.

Education and Awareness

Raising awareness about the root causes of regional disparities, economic inequalities and social injustices through education can help foster understanding and empathy among citizens. By teaching the history of these issues and their impact on different communities, individuals can become more informed and motivated to work towards solutions together. Ultimately, by addressing these challenges in a unified and inclusive manner, a stronger sense of national unity and patriotism can be achieved.

Nationalism vs. Patriotism: Finding the Right Balance for a Developing Nation like India

Nationalism and patriotism are two powerful sentiments that influence the socio-political and cultural landscape of a nation. While they are often used interchangeably, they embody different ideologies and implications. For a developing nation like India, understanding and balancing these sentiments is crucial for fostering unity, progress and stability. This part of the chapter explores the distinctions between nationalism and patriotism[10], their implications for India and the optimal mix of both for the country's development.

Understanding Nationalism and Patriotism

Nationalism

Nationalism is the belief in the superiority and interests of one's nation over others. It often involves a strong sense of identity based on shared culture, history, language and values. Nationalism can be aggressive and exclusionary, leading to a heightened sense of pride and sometimes hostility towards other nations or groups perceived as outsiders.

Characteristics of Nationalism

Key characteristics of nationalism include:

- Emphasis on National Sovereignty: Nationalists prioritize the sovereignty and autonomy of their nation, often advocating

---

[10] *https://www.britannica.com/topic/patriotism-sociology*

for self-determination and resistance to external influences.

- Cultural Homogeneity: Nationalism tends to emphasize cultural unity and homogeneity, sometimes at the expense of minority groups and cultural diversity.

- Political Agenda: Nationalist movements often have a strong political agenda, seeking to shape national policies and identity in accordance with nationalist ideals.

Patriotism

Patriotism, on the other hand, is the love and devotion to one's country. It involves a sense of pride in the nation's achievements and values, coupled with a commitment to contribute positively to its development. Unlike nationalism, patriotism is inclusive and focuses on the well-being of the nation without necessarily devaluing others.

Characteristic of Patriotism

Key characteristics of patriotism include:

- **Civic Responsibility:** Patriots actively participate in civic duties, such as voting, community service and public discourse, to contribute to national progress.

- **Inclusive Pride:** Patriotic sentiments are inclusive, celebrating the nation's diversity and cultural richness.

- **Constructive Criticism:** Patriots are willing to acknowledge and address their country's shortcomings, striving for continuous improvement.

Implications for India

Nationalism in India

Nationalism has played a significant role in India's history, particularly during the struggle for independence from British colonial rule. Mahatma Gandhi, Jawaharlal Nehru led the Congress unarmed movement and another side armed movement led by Netaji Subhash Ch. Bose led the Indian Nationalist Movement, which was crucial in organizing the populace and achieving independence. However, post-independence, the expression of nationalism has evolved and, at times, taken on exclusionary and divisive forms.

Positive aspects of nationalism in India include:

- **National Unity:** Nationalism can foster a sense of unity and collective identity, which is essential for a diverse nation like India.

- **Cultural Revival:** Nationalist movements often emphasize the revival and preservation of indigenous culture, traditions and languages.

Negative aspects of nationalism in India include:

- **Exclusionary Practices:** Aggressive nationalism can marginalize minority groups and exacerbate social divisions.

- **Political Exploitation**: Nationalism can be exploited for political gain, leading to polarized and divisive rhetoric.

Patriotism in India

Patriotism in India is characterized by a deep love for the country and a commitment to its progress and well-being. It is inclusive, embracing the nation's diversity and promoting unity and social harmony.

 Positive aspects of patriotism in India include:

-**Civic Engagement:** Patriotic citizens are more likely to engage in civic activities, contributing to the democratic process and community development.

- **Social Cohesion:** Patriotism promotes social cohesion by celebrating India's cultural diversity and fostering mutual respect and understanding.

-    **Constructive Progress:** Patriotic sentiments encourage constructive criticism and efforts to address national challenges, driving continuous improvement.

Negative Aspects of Patriotism

Negative aspects of patriotism in India include:

- **Complacency:** Excessive pride in national achievements can sometimes lead to complacency and resistance to change or criticism.

The Best Mix for a Developing Nation Like India

Finding the right balance between nationalism and patriotism is crucial for India's development. A constructive mix can harness the positive aspects of both sentiments while mitigating their negative implications.

Promoting Inclusive Nationalism

Inclusive nationalism can foster a sense of unity and collective identity without marginalizing minority groups. It should emphasize cultural revival and pride in national achievements while ensuring that all citizens feel valued and included.

Fostering Constructive Patriotism

Constructive patriotism encourages active civic engagement, social cohesion and continuous improvement. It involves a commitment to the nation's well-being while embracing diversity and promoting social harmony.

Balancing Both Sentiments

Balancing nationalism and patriotism require a nuanced approach that leverages their strengths and mitigates their weaknesses. This balance can be achieved through the following strategies:

1. Leadership and Rhetoric: National leaders play a crucial role in shaping national sentiments. They should promote inclusive nationalism and constructive patriotism through their rhetoric and actions, setting an example for the citizens.

2. Media and Communication: The media has a powerful influence on public sentiment. Media outlets should highlight stories that promote unity, inclusivity and national pride, while avoiding divisive and exclusionary narratives.

3. Policy and Governance: Government policies should reflect a balance between nationalism and patriotism. Policies should promote national interests while ensuring social and economic inclusion. Transparent and accountable governance can build trust and foster patriotic sentiments.

4. Community Engagement: Community engagement initiatives can promote both nationalism and patriotism by encouraging citizens to participate in activities that benefit the nation and their communities. This can include volunteering, community service and local governance.

5. Education and Awareness: Education systems should promote both national pride and civic responsibility. This can be achieved through a curriculum that includes national history, cultural studies and civic education.

Case Studies and Examples

Mahatma Gandhi: A Model of Balanced Patriotism and Nationalism

Mahatma Gandhi exemplified a balance between nationalism and patriotism. His nationalist efforts to achieve independence from British rule were grounded in a deep love for India and a commitment to its people. Gandhi's inclusive approach, emphasizing non-violence and unity, fostered social cohesion and national pride. His legacy demonstrates that it is possible to be a nationalist and a patriot simultaneously, advocating for national sovereignty while promoting inclusivity and social harmony.

Singapore: Fostering National Unity and Civic Responsibility

Singapore provides a valuable example of balancing nationalism and patriotism. The country's leadership has successfully promoted a strong sense of national identity and pride while fostering civic responsibility and social cohesion. Policies emphasizing multiculturalism and meritocracy have helped create an inclusive national narrative. National Service, compulsory for all male citizens, fosters a sense of duty and commitment to the nation, blending patriotic sentiments with a strong national identity.

Challenges to Achieving the Right Balance

Despite the potential benefits, achieving the right balance between nationalism and patriotism poses several challenges:

1.Political Polarization: Political polarization can exacerbate nationalist sentiments and undermine efforts to foster inclusive patriotism. Overcoming this requires bipartisan efforts and a focus on common national goals.

2. Cultural and Regional Diversity: India's vast cultural and regional diversity can make it challenging to promote a unified national identity. Balancing regional identities with a sense of national unity requires sensitive and inclusive policies.

3. Economic Disparities: Economic inequalities can lead to social divisions and undermine national unity. Addressing these disparities through equitable policies is essential for fostering inclusive nationalism and patriotism.

For a developing nation like India, balancing nationalism and patriotism is crucial for fostering unity, progress and stability. Inclusive nationalism can promote national pride and unity, while constructive patriotism encourages active civic engagement and social cohesion. By leveraging the strengths of both sentiments and addressing their potential pitfalls, India can build a more united, resilient and progressive nation.

Strategies to achieve this balance include promoting inclusive cultural education, implementing inclusive policies, encouraging public participation and fostering leadership that exemplifies the values of both nationalism and patriotism. Learning from historical figures and contemporary examples like Singapore, India can navigate the complexities of its diverse society and achieve sustainable development.

In conclusion, enhancing both nationalism and patriotism in a balanced and inclusive manner is essential for India's journey towards becoming a more developed and cohesive nation. By fostering a sense of pride and responsibility among its citizens, India can harness the full potential of its people and achieve its aspirations on the global stage.

India's poverty rate is half of what it was 15 years ago—415 million less people below poverty line—according to UN
Chapter-10
Can a Nation Think About Patriotism When the Majority of People Live Below the Poverty Line?
@dibyenduchoudhury

Chapter 10: Case Study- India

Can a Nation Think About Patriotism When the Majority of People Live Below the Poverty Line?

Patriotism, the love and devotion to one's country, is often regarded as a fundamental component of national unity and identity. However, fostering patriotism in a nation where a significant portion of the population lives below the poverty line presents unique challenges. Here we explore whether a nation can genuinely focus on cultivating patriotism when widespread poverty persists and examine the interplay between economic well-being and national pride. It also considers the role of government policies, social initiatives and community engagement in bridging this gap.

The Intersection of Poverty and Patriotism

Understanding Poverty and its Impact

Poverty is a condition characterized by severe deprivation of basic human needs, including food, safe drinking water, sanitation facilities, health, shelter, education and information. In countries where a substantial part of the population lives in poverty, daily survival takes precedence over broader societal concerns such as national pride.

Living in poverty affects individuals' capacity to participate fully in societal and civic activities. When basic needs are unmet, concerns about national identity and patriotism can seem abstract and irrelevant. Furthermore, poverty often leads to feelings of marginalization and disillusionment with the state, further eroding any sense of patriotism.

The Concept of Patriotism

Patriotism involves a sense of pride in and loyalty to one's country. It manifests in various forms, from supporting national sports teams to participating in national holidays and political processes. For patriotism to thrive, citizens need to feel a sense of belongingness and pride in their country. This is challenging when daily life is a struggle for survival.

Education, economic stability, cultural heritage and political leadership are a few factors that can affect patriotism. When a significant portion of the population is impoverished, these factors are often compromised, making it difficult to cultivate a widespread sense of patriotism.

Economic Well-being as a Foundation for Patriotism

The Importance of Economic Stability

Economic stability is a critical foundation for fostering patriotism. When citizens have access to basic needs and opportunities for economic advancement, they are more likely to develop[11] a sense of pride and loyalty to their country. Economic stability provides the resources necessary for individuals to participate in civic life and contribute to national development.

Case Study: India

India presents a relevant case study for examining the relationship between poverty and patriotism. Despite its rapid economic growth, India continues to grapple with significant poverty. According to recent estimates, a considerable percentage of the population still lives below the poverty line, struggling with issues such as malnutrition, lack of education and inadequate healthcare.

---

[11] https://www.edweek.org/policy-politics/opinion-the-importance-of-diverse-perspectives-and-how-to-foster-them/2018/11

In such a context, fostering patriotism requires addressing the underlying economic disparities. The Indian government has implemented various policies and programs aimed at alleviating poverty and promoting inclusive growth. Schemes like the Mahatma Gandhi National Rural Employment Guarantee Act (MGNREGA)[12], Pradhan Mantri Jan Dhan Yojana (PMJDY) aim to provide financial stability and employment opportunities to the poorest sections of society.

In recent years, the Government of India has launched a series of comprehensive initiatives aimed at uplifting poverty-ridden populations, particularly in rural areas and integrating them into the mainstream economy. These initiatives are designed to address various facets of poverty, from providing basic necessities to enhancing livelihoods and ensuring overall well-being. Among these initiatives, UJALA, PM Awas Yojana, Swachh Bharat Abhiyan, PM

---

[12] *https://ruralindiaonline.org/ta/library/resource/the-mahatma-gandhi-national-rural-employment-guarantee-act-2005/*

Vishwakarma Yojana and others stand out for their impactful contributions to rural development and poverty alleviation.

UJALA [13](Unnat Jyoti by Affordable LEDs for All)

The UJALA program, launched in 2015, aims to promote energy efficiency by distributing affordable LED bulbs to households across India. This initiative not only reduces electricity bills for the poor but also contributes to environmental sustainability by lowering carbon emissions. By replacing traditional incandescent bulbs with energy-efficient LEDs, UJALA has significantly reduced household energy consumption and brought affordable lighting to millions of rural homes. The widespread adoption of LED lighting has improved the quality of life in rural areas, allowing children to study in the evening and families to engage in economic activities after dark.

Pradhan Mantri Awas Yojana (PMAY) - "Housing for All"

---

[13]*https://en.wikipedia.org/wiki/Unnat_Jyoti_by_Affordable _LEDs_for_All*

The Pradhan Mantri Awas Yojana, launched in 2015, aims to provide affordable housing to the urban and rural poor by 2022. The scheme offers financial assistance to beneficiaries for constructing or renovating their homes. In rural areas, PMAY-Gramin focuses on constructing pucca houses with basic amenities, ensuring that even the poorest families have access to safe and dignified living conditions. The program also emphasizes the use of sustainable and eco-friendly construction technologies, contributing to the broader goals of environmental sustainability and resilience against natural disasters.

Swachh Bharat Abhiyan (Clean India Mission)

Swachh Bharat Abhiyan, launched in 2014, is a nationwide campaign aimed at eliminating open defecation and improving solid waste management. The mission focuses on constructing toilets, promoting sanitation practices and ensuring cleanliness in both urban and rural areas. By providing access to proper sanitation facilities, Swachh Bharat Abhiyan has significantly improved public health, reduced the incidence of waterborne diseases and enhanced the quality of life for rural populations. The campaign also involves extensive awareness programs to educate communities about the importance of hygiene and sanitation, fostering behavioural change and community participation.

Pradhan Mantri Vishwakarma Kaushal Samman (PM Vishwakarma Yojana)

The PM Vishwakarma Yojana, recently introduced, is aimed at recognizing and supporting traditional artisans and craftsmen, who often belong to marginalized communities. This initiative provides financial assistance, training and marketing support to help artisans improve their skills, increase their productivity and access wider markets. By empowering traditional craftsmen, the scheme not only preserves India's rich cultural heritage but also provides sustainable livelihoods to rural populations, reducing poverty and promoting economic inclusion.

Other Notable Initiatives

Pradhan Mantri Jan Dhan Yojana (PMJDY)

Launched in 2014, the PMJDY aims to provide universal access to banking facilities, with at least one basic banking account for every household. The scheme also includes financial literacy programs and access to credit and insurance. By promoting financial inclusion, PMJDY empowers rural populations to save, invest and secure their financial futures.

Deen Dayal Upadhyaya Grameen Kaushalya Yojana (DDU-GKY)[14]

DDU-GKY focuses on enhancing the employability of rural youth by providing skill development training aligned with industry requirements. The program aims to bridge the gap between rural talent and market demand, creating job opportunities and reducing rural-urban migration.

Pradhan Mantri Ujjwala Yojana (PMUY)

Launched in 2016, PMUY aims to provide clean cooking fuel to rural households by distributing LPG connections to families below the poverty line. This initiative addresses health issues caused by indoor air pollution from traditional cooking methods

---

[14] *https://www.myscheme.gov.in/schemes/ddugku*

and promotes gender equality by reducing the time and effort women spend on gathering firewood.

Comprehensive Impact and Future Prospects

These initiatives collectively represent a multifaceted approach to poverty alleviation, addressing various dimensions of rural deprivation. By improving access to basic amenities, enhancing livelihoods and promoting sustainable practices, the Government of India[15] is working towards integrating rural populations into the mainstream economy and ensuring inclusive development.

The success of these programs lies in their ability to create a synergistic impact. For instance, providing affordable housing through PMAY complements the goals of Swachh Bharat Abhiyan by ensuring that new homes are equipped with proper

---

[15] https://www.uschamber.com/on-demand/economy/how-indian-businesses-will-benefit-from-global-supply-chain-realignment

sanitation facilities. Similarly, skill development initiatives like DDU-GKY enhance the employability of rural youth, making them beneficiaries of schemes like PMJDY, which promote financial inclusion.

Going forward, it is essential to ensure the effective implementation and monitoring of these programs to maximize their impact. Continuous efforts to involve local communities, improve infrastructure and enhance the delivery of services will be crucial in achieving the overarching goal of poverty alleviation and economic inclusion. Additionally, fostering partnerships with non-governmental organizations, private sector stakeholders and international agencies can provide the necessary support and resources to scale these initiatives further.

In conclusion, the Government of India's recent initiatives, such as UJALA, PM Awas Yojana, Swachh Bharat Abhiyan, PM Vishwakarma Yojana and others, represent a comprehensive strategy to uplift poverty-ridden populations, particularly in rural areas. By addressing basic needs, promoting economic opportunities and fostering sustainable practices, these programs aim to integrate marginalized communities into the mainstream economy and pave the way for a more inclusive and prosperous future.

These initiatives have had varying degrees of success in improving the livelihoods of those living in poverty, but more needs to be done to ensure sustainable and long-term economic development for all of India's citizens. Addressing the root causes of economic disparities, such as lack of access to education, healthcare and basic infrastructure, will be crucial in creating a more equitable society[16]. It is imperative that the government continues to prioritize poverty alleviation efforts and work towards creating a society where all individuals have equal opportunities to thrive.

---

[16] https://www.mdpi.com/2071-1050/15/13/10682

Government Policies and Initiatives

Social Welfare Programs

Government policies and social welfare programs play a crucial role in bridging the gap between poverty and patriotism. By addressing the immediate needs of the impoverished population, these programs can create a foundation upon which a sense of national pride can be built.

For example, in India, the Public Distribution System (PDS) provides subsidized food to millions of low-income families, ensuring food security. The Mid-Day Meal Scheme aims to improve nutritional levels among schoolchildren while also encouraging school attendance. These programs not only address basic needs but also foster a sense of inclusion and belonging among beneficiaries, laying the groundwork for patriotic sentiments.

Education and Awareness

Education is a powerful tool for cultivating patriotism. By providing access to quality education, governments can empower citizens with the knowledge and skills necessary to contribute to national development. Educational programs that include lessons on national history, values and civic responsibilities can instil a sense of pride and loyalty to the country. The revised National Education Policy (2020) was envisaged to not only improve the quality of education but also promote a sense of patriotism among students. By incorporating lessons on India's rich cultural heritage, diverse history and values of unity and diversity, the policy aims to instil a deep sense of national pride in the younger generation. Through education and awareness, the government hopes to create a more cohesive and patriotic society that is committed to the progress and prosperity of the nation.

In India, initiatives such as the Right to Education Act (RTE) aim to provide free and compulsory education to all children, ensuring that even those from impoverished backgrounds have the opportunity to learn and grow. Additionally, programs like Digital India seek to bridge the digital divide and provide access to information and technology, further empowering citizens.

Community Engagement and Grassroots Movements

Role of Civil Society

Civil society organizations and grassroots movements can play a significant role in fostering patriotism among impoverished communities. By working directly with these communities, they can address immediate needs while also promoting a sense of national identity and pride.

For instance, non-governmental organizations (NGOs) in India have been instrumental in implementing programs related to health, education and livelihoods. These organizations often work in collaboration with government agencies to ensure that resources reach those in need. By involving community members in these initiatives, NGOs can foster a sense of ownership and pride in their contributions to national development.

Community-Based Programs

Community-based programs that promote local culture and traditions can also foster patriotism. By celebrating local heritage and involving community members in cultural activities, these programs can create a sense of pride and belonging.

In India, programs that promote traditional crafts, arts and festivals play a crucial role in preserving cultural heritage while also providing economic opportunities for local communities. Initiatives like the Khadi and Village Industries Commission (KVIC) promote the production of traditional handwoven fabrics, providing livelihoods to rural artisans while also promoting national pride in indigenous crafts.

The Role of Leadership and Governance

Transparent and Inclusive Governance

Effective leadership and transparent governance are essential for fostering patriotism, especially in nations grappling with poverty. When citizens trust their leaders and believe that the government is working in their best interests, they are more likely to develop a sense of loyalty and pride in their country.

Promoting Inclusive Policies

Inclusive policies that address the needs of all citizens, regardless of their socio-economic status, are crucial for fostering patriotism. By ensuring that marginalized communities have access to resources and opportunities, governments can create a more equitable society where all citizens feel valued and included.

In India, policies aimed at promoting social inclusion, such as reservations for Scheduled Castes, Scheduled Tribes and Other Backward Classes in education and employment, have been instrumental in addressing historical inequalities and promoting social mobility.

Inspiring Leadership

Inspiring leadership that embodies national values and ideals can also foster patriotism. Leaders who demonstrate integrity, dedication and a commitment to national development can serve as role models for citizens, inspiring them to contribute to the country's progress.

Leaders like Mahatma Gandhi, Jawaharlal Nehru and Dr. APJ Abdul Kalam are revered in India for their contributions to the nation's development and their embodiment of national values. Their leadership has inspired generations of Indians to work towards a better future for their country.

Addressing Structural Inequalities

Economic Reforms

Addressing structural inequalities through economic reforms is crucial for reducing poverty and fostering patriotism. Reforms that promote inclusive growth, create employment opportunities and ensure access to basic services can help lift people out of poverty and create a more equitable society.

Land Reforms

Land reforms that address issues of land ownership and distribution can play a significant role in reducing poverty and promoting social justice. Ensuring that marginalized communities have access to land and resources can empower them economically and foster a sense of belonging and pride in their country.

In India, land reform policies aimed at redistributing land to landless farmers have been implemented in various states, with varying degrees of success. These policies aim to address historical inequalities and promote rural development.

Access to Financial Services

Access to financial services is essential for economic empowerment and poverty reduction. Ensuring that marginalized communities have access to banking services, credit and insurance can help them build assets, manage risks and improve their economic well-being.

In India, initiatives like the Pradhan Mantri Jan Dhan Yojana (PMJDY) aim to provide financial inclusion by opening bank accounts for millions of unbanked individuals, providing them with access to financial services and social security schemes.

The Role of Culture and Heritage

Promoting Cultural Heritage

Promoting and preserving cultural heritage can foster a sense of national identity and pride among citizens. By celebrating the country's rich cultural diversity, governments and communities can create a sense of unity and belonging.

Celebrating National Festivals

National festivals and cultural events provide opportunities for citizens to come together and celebrate their shared heritage. These events can foster a sense of pride and unity, transcending socio-economic differences.

In India, festivals like Diwali, Eid, Christmas and Independence Day are celebrated across the country, bringing people from different backgrounds together in a spirit of unity and celebration. These festivals provide a platform for promoting national values and fostering a sense of belonging.

Supporting Traditional Arts and Crafts

Supporting traditional arts and crafts can provide economic opportunities for marginalized communities while also promoting cultural heritage. By providing training, marketing support and financial assistance to artisans, governments can empower these communities economically and foster a sense of pride in their cultural contributions.

In India, initiatives like the Handloom and Handicrafts Development Programme aim to support traditional artisans by providing them with access to resources, training and markets. These programs help preserve cultural heritage while also promoting economic development.

Conclusion

Fostering patriotism in a nation where a significant portion of the population lives below the poverty line presents unique challenges. However, it is not an insurmountable task. By addressing the root causes of poverty and promoting inclusive growth, governments can create a foundation upon which a sense of national pride can be built.

Key factors in improving patriotism include providing access to quality education, implementing social welfare programs, promoting inclusive policies and supporting cultural heritage. Community engagement and grassroots movements also play a crucial role in fostering a sense of belonging and pride among marginalized communities.

Effective leadership and transparent governance are essential for building trust and inspiring citizens to contribute to national development. By addressing structural inequalities and promoting economic empowerment, governments can create a more equitable society where all citizens feel valued and important. Furthermore, investing in infrastructure and healthcare services can greatly improve the overall well-being of the population and reduce disparities in access to resources. By prioritizing the needs of marginalized groups and listening to their concerns, governments can ensure that policies are inclusive and beneficial for all. Ultimately, creating a society where every individual feels empowered and supported is key to achieving sustainable development and prosperity for all.

All Non-Fictions Books (Education and Business Management related): Available online with www.amazon.in

Other Books of the Author

Dr. Dibyendu Choudhury, one of India's eminent Management Gurus and mythologists, offers an interesting look at the top 25 personalities modern organizations may need in their leadership positions post pandemic. He draws on stories from the Mahabharata and the Ramayana. Businesses

often need visionary leaders with an entrepreneurial

spirit to steer them through challenging times. In the wake of the pandemic, most businesses don't know how to pick a leader who can successfully communicate, inspire workers, and strike the correct balance between strictness and compassion. This applies to any workplace i.e., Micro to Medium Enterprises and even large corporates. This is applied to any workplace. Dibyendu demonstrates the timeless management lessons that may be gleaned from stories written thousands of years ago. Be the Leader, Not the Boss! 25 Secrets to Being an Entrepreneurial Leader with Insights from Mythology draws on mythological figures and contemporary stories to reveal timeless truths about what it takes to be an effective and innovative leader. All his books available in Amazon India Site.

All the books are available in www.amazon.com

View the Author's Profile
https://www.amazon.com/stores/author/B0B9
KZPBHY/about

Fictions

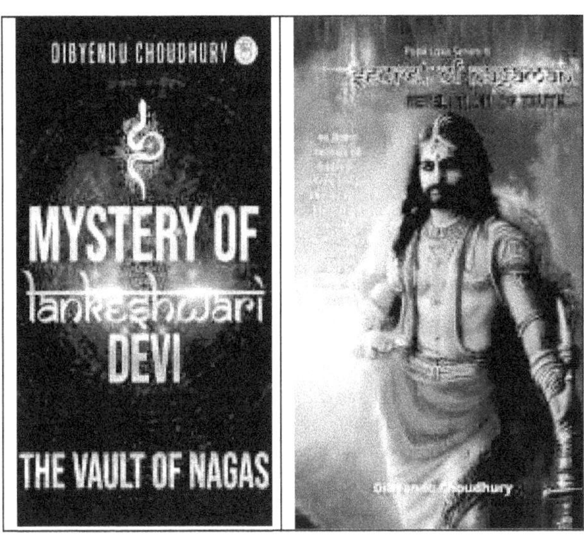

The Patal Loka Series by Dibyendu Choudhury

Dibyendu Choudhury's fictional series "Patal Loka" is a captivating five-part saga that delves deep into the mysteries of Hindu mythology, blending elements of fiction, adventure, and mysticism. Since its inception in 2023, the series has released two books, with a new instalment scheduled to come out each year.

Book 3: "The Secret of Bhoothnath Temple: Gates of Patal Loka" (2025)

The third book introduces readers to the mystical world of Patal Loka, a hidden realm intertwined with Hindu mythology. The story follows a group of adventurers who stumble upon ancient secrets that could change the course of history. As they navigate through the enigmatic world, they encounter gods, demons, and mythical creatures, unravelling a tapestry of mysteries that challenge their understanding of reality.

Book 4: "The Mystery of Kailash: Serpent's Curse (2026)"

In the fourth instalment, the protagonists continue their journey deeper into Patal Loka. They face new challenges, including the wrath of a cursed serpent deity that threatens to unleash chaos upon the world. The adventure intensifies as they seek to break the curse and protect the balance between the realms. Along the way, they uncover more secrets about their own destinies and the ancient prophecies that guide their path.

The "Patal Loka" series has been praised for its intricate and fast paced storytelling, rich character development, and immersive portrayal of Hindu mythology. Dibyendu Choudhury's masterful blend of adventure and mysticism keeps readers eagerly anticipating each new release.

With three more books to come, readers can look forward to further exploring the depths of Patal Loka, discovering more about its mysteries, and witnessing the epic saga unfold. As each year brings a new chapter, the series promises to remain a thrilling and thought-provoking journey into the heart of Hindu myth and legend.

Web References:

(1) There are many ways to be patriotic - The McCourtney Institute for .... https://democracy.psu.edu/poll-report-archive/there-are-many-ways-to-be-patriotic/.

(2) Patriotism | Nationalism, Social Identity & Loyalty | Britannica. https://www.britannica.com/topic/patriotism-sociology.

(3) Requirements to Increase Patriotism Unit 5 Patriotism. https://elearn.moe.gov.et/storage/civics/text%20book/G-10/Unit%205.pdf.

(4) The role of organizational citizenship behavior and patriotism in .... https://www.frontiersin.org/articles/10.3389/fpsyg.2022.99 7643/full.

(5) 6 Simple Ways to be More Patriotic - The Bucket List Project. https://www.ericgamble.com/6-simple-ways-to-be-more-patriotic-us-flag/.

(6) Why Is Patriotism Important? (10 Reasons) - Enlightio. https://enlightio.com/why-is-patriotism-important.

(7) Patriotism: meaning, types and importance - Ritu's Academy. https://ritusacademy.com/patriotism-meaning-types-and-importance/.

(8) Importance of Patriotism Essay for Students and Children in English.

https://www.aplustopper.com/importance-of-patriotism-essay/.

(9) There are many ways to be patriotic - The McCourtney Institute for .... https://democracy.psu.edu/poll-report-archive/there-are-many-ways-to-be-patriotic/.

(10) Patriotism | Nationalism, Social Identity & Loyalty | Britannica. https://www.britannica.com/topic/patriotism-sociology.

(11) Requirements to Increase Patriotism Unit 5 Patriotism. https://elearn.moe.gov.et/storage/civics/text%20book/G-10/Unit%205.pdf.

(12) The role of organizational citizenship behavior and patriotism in .... https://www.frontiersin.org/articles/10.3389/fpsyg.2022.997643/full.

(13) 6 Simple Ways to be More Patriotic - The Bucket List Project. https://www.ericgamble.com/6-simple-ways-to-be-more-patriotic-us-flag/.

(14) Why Is Patriotism Important? (10 Reasons) - Enlightio. https://enlightio.com/why-is-patriotism-important.

(15) Patriotism: meaning, types and importance - Ritu's Academy. https://ritusacademy.com/patriotism-meaning-types-and-importance/.

(16) Importance of Patriotism Essay for Students and Children in English. https://www.aplustopper.com/importance-of-patriotism-essay/.

(17) Patriotism | Nationalism, Social Identity & Loyalty | Britannica. https://www.britannica.com/topic/patriotism-sociology.

(18) Initiatives taken by the government to boost manufacturing. https://pib.gov.in/PressReleaseIframePage.aspx?PRID=1882145.

(19) Development Programmes and Key Initiatives in India | IIG. https://indiainvestmentgrid.gov.in/schemes.

(20) Explained: What government can do to revive India's ... - India Today. https://www.indiatoday.in/business/story/explained-what-government-can-do-to-revive-india-s-shrinking-economy-1719679-2020-09-08.

(21) Price Volume Mix (PVM) for Gross Margin Variance Analysis. https://businessintelligist.com/2020/04/26/price-volume-mix-pvm-for-gross-margin-variance-analysis/.

(22) New York City Enacts New Gender-Motivated Violence Act. https://www.kmm.com/new-york-city-enacts-new-gender-motivated-violence-act/.

(23) A recipe for a successful nation - The Conversation. https://theconversation.com/a-recipe-for-a-successful-nation-86516.

(24) Value Added by Industry: Manufacturing as a Percentage of GDP. https://fred.stlouisfed.org/series/VAPGDPMA.

(25) Value added to GDP by manufacturing U.S. 2022 | Statista. https://www.statista.com/statistics/1262893/value-added-us-manufacturing/.

(26) How To Calculate Value Added (With Examples) | Indeed.com. https://www.indeed.com/career-advice/career-development/how-to-calculate-value-added.

(27) Manufacturing, value added (% of GDP) - United States | Data. https://data.worldbank.org/indicator/NV.IND.MANF.ZS?locations=US.

(28) Global manufacturing scorecard: How the US compares to 18 other nations .... https://www.brookings.edu/articles/global-manufacturing-scorecard-how-the-us-compares-to-18-other-nations/.

(29) List of countries by labour productivity - Wikipedia. https://en.wikipedia.org/wiki/List_of_countries_by_labour_productivity.

(30) The U.S. productivity slowdown: an economy-wide and industry-level ....
https://www.bls.gov/opub/mlr/2021/article/the-us-productivity-slowdown-the-economy-wide-and-industry-level-analysis.htm.

(31) Productivity: output per hour worked - Our World in Data. https://ourworldindata.org/grapher/labor-productivity-per-hour-pennworldtable.

(32) Employee Productivity vs. Hours Worked: What's the Difference?. https://humanyze.com/blog-employee-productivity-vs-hours-worked-whats-the-difference/.

(33) Annual working hours vs. labor productivity - Our World in Data. https://ourworldindata.org/grapher/productivity-vs-annual-hours-worked.

(34) Do workers in richer countries work longer hours?. https://ourworldindata.org/rich-poor-working-hours.

(35) These Are the Most Productive Countries in the World | Time. https://time.com/4621185/worker-productivity-countries/.

(36) The Benefits and Challenges of Implementing Technology in HR Management ....
https://talent500.co/blog/the-benefits-and-challenges-of-implementing-technology-in-hr-management/.

(37) 8 common HR technology challenges and how to overcome them. https://www.insperity.com/blog/hr-technology-challenges/.

(38) 9 Common Workday Implementation Challenges - Surety Systems. https://www.suretysystems.com/insights/9-common-workday-implementation-challenges/.

(39) Strategies for Managing Work Hours Effectively: - eLeaP. https://www.eleapsoftware.com/glossary/strategies-for-managing-work-hours-effectively/.

(40) The Increasing Role of Technology Integration in Time Management. https://simpleprogrammer.com/time-management-apps/.

(41) How can technology help with time management? - Enterprise Times. https://www.enterprisetimes.co.uk/2018/10/16/how-can-technology-help-with-time-management/.

(42) The Role of Technology in Modern Performance Management - Evalflow. https://www.evalflow.com/blog/the-role-of-technology-in-modern-performance-management.

(43) Working Time • Business & Human Rights Navigator. https://bhr-navigator.unglobalcompact.org/issues/working-time/.

(44) Poor working conditions are main global employment challenge. https://www.ilo.org/global/about-the-ilo/newsroom/news/WCMS_670171/lang--en/index.htm.

(45) HR issues in multinational companies: Tackling challenges of IHRM - HiBob. https://www.hibob.com/blog/hr-challenges-in-multinational-companies/.

(46) Labour market trends: longer-term challenges and impact of crises. https://www.un.org/development/desa/dspd/wp-content/uploads/sites/22/2022/06/Verick_Labour-market-trends-longer-term-challenges-and-impact-of-crises.pdf.

(47) Working Hours - World Bank Group. https://www.worldbank.org/en/research/employing-workers/data/working-hours.

(48) How do my working hours affect my productivity? | World Economic Forum. https://www.weforum.org/agenda/2021/09/teams-productivity-work-hours/.

(49) Understanding worker productivity and how it relates to economic growth .... https://www.thehindu.com/business/Economy/understanding-worker-productivity-and-how-it-relates-to-economic-growth-explained/article67490775.ece.

(50) Worker's Productivity: Long working hours - InsightsIAS.
https://www.insightsonindia.com/2023/10/30/workers-productivity-long-working-hours/.

(51) Working Hours - Our World in Data.
https://ourworldindata.org/working-hours.

(52) Annual working hours vs. labor productivity - Our World in Data.
https://ourworldindata.org/grapher/productivity-vs-annual-hours-worked.

(53) How do my working hours affect my productivity? | World Economic Forum.
https://www.weforum.org/agenda/2021/09/teams-productivity-work-hours/.

(54) Understanding worker productivity and how it relates to economic growth ....
https://www.thehindu.com/business/Economy/understanding-worker-productivity-and-how-it-relates-to-economic-growth-explained/article67490775.ece.

(55) Worker's Productivity: Long working hours - InsightsIAS.
https://www.insightsonindia.com/2023/10/30/workers-productivity-long-working-hours/.

(56) Working Hours - Our World in Data. https://ourworldindata.org/working-hours.

(57) Annual working hours vs. labor productivity - Our World in Data. https://ourworldindata.org/grapher/productivity-vs-annual-hours-worked.

(58) How do my working hours affect my productivity? | World Economic Forum. https://www.weforum.org/agenda/2021/09/teams-productivity-work-hours/.

(59) Understanding worker productivity and how it relates to economic growth .... https://www.thehindu.com/business/Economy/understanding-worker-productivity-and-how-it-relates-to-economic-growth-explained/article67490775.ece.

(60) Worker's Productivity: Long working hours - InsightsIAS. https://www.insightsonindia.com/2023/10/30/workers-productivity-long-working-hours/.

(61) Working Hours - Our World in Data. https://ourworldindata.org/working-hours.

(62) Annual working hours vs. labor productivity - Our World in Data. https://ourworldindata.org/grapher/productivity-vs-annual-hours-worked.

(63) Narayana Murthy says Indian youth should work 70 hours ... - Times of India. https://bing.com/search?q=Narayana+Murthy+advocate+longer+work+hours+for+India%27s+Youth.

(64) Narayana Murthy says Indian youth should work 70 hours ... - Times of India. https://timesofindia.indiatimes.com/business/india-business/narayana-murthy-says-indian-youth-should-work-70-hours-a-week-not-pick-undesirable-habits-from-the-west/articleshow/104732137.cms.

(65) Bengaluru startup's twist to Narayana Murthy's 70-hour work week advice wins the internet. Watch. https://www.msn.com/en-in/news/other/bengaluru-startups-twist-to-narayana-murthys-70-hour-work-week-advice-wins-the-internet-watch/ar-BB1lGGmW.

(66) Angry Rantman's Death: His last rant was against NR Narayana Murthy's 70-hour work-week - What he said. https://www.msn.com/en-in/news/india/angry-rantmans-death-his-last-rant-was-against-nr-narayana-murthys-70-hour-work-week-what-he-said/ar-AA1nfvbU.

(67) Should Indian Youth Work 70 Hours A Week? Narayana Murthy's Suggestion .... https://www.oneindia.com/india/should-indian-youth-work-70-hours-a-week-narayana-murthys-suggestion-ignites-debate-on-x-3668867.html.

(68) Infosys founder Narayana Murthy says young IT workers ... - India Today. https://www.indiatoday.in/technology/news/story/infosys-founder-narayana-murthy-says-young-it-workers-should-work-70-hours-a-week-new-work-culture-is-needed-2454047-2023-10-26.

(69) Difference Between Entrepreneur and Intrapreneur. https://keydifferences.com/difference-between-entrepreneur-and-intrapreneur.html.

(70) Entrepreneur vs. Intrapreneur | GCU Blog - Grand Canyon University. https://www.gcu.edu/blog/business-management/entrepreneur-vs-intrapreneur.

(71) Difference Between Entrepreneur and Intrapreneur - Shiksha Online. https://www.shiksha.com/online-courses/articles/difference-between-entrepreneur-and-intrapreneur/.

(72) Intrapreneurship Vs Entrepreneurship - What's The Difference?. https://www.nexford.edu/insights/intrapreneurship-vs-entrepreneurship.

(73) How to motivate employees: Key factors, strategies, and examples. https://blog.jostle.me/blog/motivate-employees.

(74) 14 Simple And Effective Ways To Motivate Your Employees - Forbes.

https://bing.com/search?q=how+to+increase+achievement+
motivation+in+employees.

(75) 14 Simple And Effective Ways To Motivate Your
Employees   -   Forbes.
https://www.forbes.com/sites/forbesbusinesscouncil/2022/0
1/26/14-simple-and-effective-ways-to-motivate-your-
employees/.

(76) How to Increase Employee Motivation | Expert360.
https://expert360.com/articles/how-to-increase-employee-
motivation.

(77) 42 Tested Ways To Drastically Increase Employee
Engagement   and   Motivation.
https://blog.giftpack.ai/article/employee-engagement-and-
motivation.

(78) How to write SMART goals (with examples) -
Atlassian.
https://www.atlassian.com/blog/productivity/how-to-write-
smart-goals.

(79) Smart Definition & Meaning - Merriam-Webster.
https://www.merriam-webster.com/dictionary/smart.

(80) Smart Definition & Meaning | Britannica Dictionary.
https://www.britannica.com/dictionary/smart.

(81) SMART | definition in the Cambridge English
Dictionary.

https://dictionary.cambridge.org/us/dictionary/english/smart.

(82) What Are SMART Goals? A Guide to Using SMART Goals. https://www.masterclass.com/articles/what-are-smart-goals.

(83) SMART | English meaning - Cambridge Dictionary. https://dictionary.cambridge.org/dictionary/english/smart.

(84) SMART Goals Explained: Examples & Templates | TeamGantt. https://www.teamgantt.com/blog/smart-goals-explained-examples-and-templates.

(85) SMART goals: A step-by-step guide (with examples) - Fingerprint For Success. https://www.fingerprintforsuccess.com/blog/smart-goals.

(86) The Ultimate Guide To S.M.A.R.T. Goals - Forbes. https://www.forbes.com/advisor/business/smart-goals/.

(87) What Are SMART Goals? Examples and Templates [2024] • Asana. https://asana.com/resources/smart-goals.

(88) Achievement Motivation: Nine Ways To Use It in the Workplace - HubSpot Blog. https://blog.hubspot.com/sales/achievement-motivation.

(89) How to Motivate Yourself: 11 Tips for Self Improvement. https://www.coursera.org/articles/how-to-motivate-yourself.

(90) Achievement Motivation Training: Crucial To The Success. https://www.mentorpal.ai/blog/achievement-motivation-training-crucial-to-the-success/.

(91) Achievement Orientation: The Road Map To Success - Mentorpal Blog. https://www.mentorpal.ai/blog/achievement-orientation-the-road-map-to-success/.

(92) What Is Achievement Motivation? - Vivien Roggero. https://vivienroggero.com/blog/what-is-achievement-motivation.

(93) en.wikipedia.org. https://en.wikipedia.org/wiki/Motivation.

(95) Achievement Motivation: Nine Ways To Use It in the Workplace - HubSpot Blog. https://blog.hubspot.com/sales/achievement-motivation.

(96) Why Motivation Matters: The Key To Success For Entrepreneurs. https://www.timeetc.com/resources/how-to-achieve-more/why-motivation-matters-the-key-to-success-for-entrepreneurs.

(97) Describe briefly the role of achievement motivation in entrepreneurship.. https://byjus.com/question-answer/describe-briefly-the-role-of-achievement-motivation-in-entrepreneurship/.

(98) The Relationship of Achievement Motivation to Entrepreneurial Behavior ....
https://ecommons.cornell.edu/bitstream/handle/1813/75082
/Collins4_The_Relationship_of_Achievement_Motivation_
post_print.pdf?sequence=1.

(99) 8 ACHIEVEMENT MOTIV ATION - The National Institute of Open Schooling (NIOS).
https://nios.ac.in/media/documents/249_Enterpreneurship/E
nglish_pdf/249_Enterpreneurship_Lesson_8.pdf.

Other Internet Sources

https://www.mdpi.com/2071-1050/15/13/10682

https://fastercapital.com/topics/understanding-gross-
merchandise-value-(gmv).html

https://aaronhall.com/insights/influencing-employee-
happiness-cultivating-a-positive-work-

https://fastercapital.com/content/Diversity-and-inclusion--
Embracing-Differences--The-Power-of-Diversity-and-
Inclusion-in-Startup-Culture.html

https://classnotes.ng/lesson/national-values-patriotism/

https://quickonomics.com/terms/output-per-hour-worked/

Unleashing India's Potential: 70 Hr. Weekly Workhour

https://humanyze.com/blog-employee-productivity-vs-hours-worked-whats-the-difference/

https://talent500.co/blog/the-benefits-and-challenges-of-implementing-technology-in-hr-management/

https://www.britannica.com/topic/patriotism-sociology

https://blog.vantagecircle.com/employee-recognition-ideas/

https://ied.eu/blog/education-blog/empowering-minds-transformative-power-education/

https://aaronhall.com/insights/empowering-employees-the-role-of-technology-in-autonomy/

https://knolskape.com/blog/the-psychology-of-productivity-understanding-context-in-performance/

https://www.pib.gov.in/PressReleaseIframePage.aspx?PRID=1947211

https://trak.in/stories/make-in-india-beyond-iots-role-in-revolutionizing-manufacturing-excellence/

https://cenkuslaw.com/annoying-email-confidentiality-disclaimers/

https://www.livemint.com/economy/from-60-hours-in-2020-narayana-murthy-now-suggests-70-hour-work-week-for-youngsters-where-will-he-go-next-11698339720990.html

https://www.imd.org/blog/innovation/what-is-disruptive-innovation/

https://www.linkedin.com/advice/3/what-do-you-your-remote-team-spread-across-b2xrc

https://kindlepreneur.com/book-copyright-page-examples-ebook/

https://indianexpress.com/article/opinion/columns/narayana-murthy-and-70-hour-work-week-a-narrow-idea-of-nation-building-9009300/

https://www.linkedin.com/pulse/power-accountability-why-taking-responsibility

https://bhr-navigator.unglobalcompact.org/issues/working-time/

https://www.linkedin.com/pulse/building-culture-innovation-key-factors-success-dr-zam

https://resanskrit.com/blogs/blog-post/sanskrit-shlok-on-father-s-day

https://www.upscaleyourpotential.com/articles/productivity-how-to-work-smarter-not-harder

https://medium.com/illuminations-mirror/the-power-of-storytelling-how-narratives-shape-our-lives-9bc7a7699253

https://www.nimsme.org/news-article/raising-accelerating-msme-performance-ramp-scheme

Unleashing India's Potential: 70 Hr. Weekly
Workhour

https://www.gktoday.in/industrial-corridor-development-programme-subprogramme/

https://www.bbc.co.uk/news/world-asia-india-67269976

https://www.edweek.org/policy-politics/opinion-the-importance-of-diverse-perspectives-and-how-to-foster-them/2018/11

https://www.uschamber.com/on-demand/economy/how-indian-businesses-will-benefit-from-global-supply-chain-realignment

https://www.inboundlogistics.com/articles/sustainable-supply-chain/

https://www.linkedin.com/pulse/evolution-healthcare-prioritizing-quality-over-chris-qjove

https://publisherreport.com/writing/writing-an-effective-disclaimer-for-your-book-a-comprehensive-guide/

https://ourworldindata.org/grapher/labor-productivity-per-hour-pennworldtable

https://economictimes.indiatimes.com/small-biz/policy-trends/how-ease-of-doing-business-can-be-made-more-effective-for-entrepreneurs/articleshow/88729965.cms

https://www.datasecurityintegrations.com/best-practices/ensuring-compliance-international-data-protection/

https://www.linkedin.com/pulse/stepping-out-your-comfort-zone-unlocking-gimpf

https://timesofindia.indiatimes.com/business/india-business/narayana-murthy-says-indian-youth-should-work-70-hours-a-week-not-pick-undesirable-habits-from-the-west/articleshow/104732137.cms

https://www.cgtstaffing.com/resources/boost-employee-morale/

https://ritusacademy.com/patriotism-meaning-types-and-importance/

https://digest.myhq.in/make-in-india-scheme/

https://www.cabkgoyal.com/indian-footwear-and-leather-development-programme-ifldp/

https://www.mckinsey.com/mhi/our-insights/working-nine-to-thrive

https://www.linkedin.com/pulse/striking-right-balance-working-hours-productivity-samah-nasr-qxkff

https://www.researchgate.net/profile/Elaheh-Yadegaridehkordi/publication/341190360_COMRAP_2018/links/5eb2ec0b45851523bd4708f1/ COMRAP-2018.pdf

https://www.ndtv.com/india-news/narayana-murthy-says-western-friends-nris-agree-with-70-hour-work-advice-4803447

Unleashing India's Potential: 70 Hr. Weekly Workhour

https://www.greatplacetowork.com/resources/blog/employee-training-development-benefits-planning

https://www.cnn.com/india-infosys-founder-work-hours-success-intl-hnk/index.html

https://www.linkedin.com/pulse/smart-goals-strategic-approach-achieving-success-jan-jarko-nt8xf

https://pib.gov.in/PressReleaseIframePage.aspx?PRID=1988824

https://www.clearias.com/national-logistics-policy/

https://blog.jostle.me/blog/motivate-employees

https://keydifferences.com/difference-between-entrepreneur-and-intrapreneur.html

https://vivekavani.com/swami-vivekananda-quotes-guru-teacher/

https://woodruffsawyer.com/insights/eap-supports-mental-health

https://www.studyiq.com/articles/skill-india-mission/

https://mohua.gov.in/upload/uploadfiles/files/TPQMA_Guideline_PMAY(U).pdf

https://thehill.com/opinion/technology/4600390-dont-believe-the-naysayers-hybrid-remote-work-is-improving-employees-mental-health/

https://www.linkedin.com/pulse/strategic-partnerships-accelerating-growth-through-collaborative

https://www.drishtiias.com/mains-practice-question/question-7954

https://www.sopact.com/guides/smart-metrics

https://whatisthedifferences.com/what-is-the-difference-between-entrepreneur-and-intrapreneur/

https://zeenews.india.com/companies/70-hrs-workweek-row-sudha-murthy-defends-husband-narayana-murthy-says-he-has-worked-80-t0-90-hrs-a-week-2682113.html

https://getriskmanager.com/risk-taking-embrace-opportunities-navigate-threats/

https://www.linkedin.com/advice/0/heres-how-you-can-create-comprehensive-feedback-u3rgf

https://pib.gov.in/PressReleseDetailm.aspx?PRID=1947509

https://www.legalserviceindia.com/legal/article-10803-critical-analysis-of-right-to-education-act-2009.html

https://www.ncbi.nlm.nih.gov/home/about/policies/

https://www.coursehero.com/file/235251292/Patriotismdocx/

https://www.mindlessmag.com/post/why-prioritizing-employee-well-being-is-a-major-boon

https://www.linkedin.com/pulse/embracing-unknown-power-taking-risks-stepping-beyond

https://ambition-in-motion.com/blog/how-to-teach-employees-to-set-smart-goals

https://quickonomics.com/terms/entrepreneur/

https://aroraias.com/history/what-is-nationalism-nationalism-in-india-arora-ias-concept/

https://link.springer.com/article/10.1007/s10668-016-9790-y

https://en.wikipedia.org/wiki/Gross_value_added

https://dcf.fm/blogs/vision/k-mission-vision

https://sscm.uphq.in/Home/MissionSmartCity

https://www.pando.com/blog-post/build-employee-commitment-to-growth-through-a-new-paradigm-in-employee-performance

https://www.culturemonkey.io/employee-engagement/employee-recognition-examples/

https://www.outbackteambuilding.com/blog/random-acts-of-kindness-day-ideas/

https://blogdo.vantagecircle.com/blog/autonomy-in-the-workplace/

https://www.forbes.com/sites/forbescommunicationscounci
l/2024/02/07/competitive-advantage-the-key-to-business-
success/

https://www.bizjournals.com/boston/news/2018/08/02/pres
s-play-five-years-later-john-henry-is-still.html

https://dollarsenseinsights.com/entrepreneur-and-
intrapreneur-difference/

https://ourworldindata.org/extreme-poverty-in-brief

https://ruralindiaonline.org/ta/library/resource/the-
mahatma-gandhi-national-rural-employment-guarantee-act-
2005/

https://en.wikipedia.org/wiki/Pradhan_Mantri_Jan_Dhan_
Yojana

https://www.hindustantimes.com/india-news/sudha-murty-
narayana-murthy-70-hour-work-debate-work-is-holiday-
101705073402702.html

https://www.linkedin.com/pulse/formula-success-hard-
work-dedication-ananya-johri/

https://cepr.org/voxeu/columns/circular-relationship-
between-productivity-and-hours-worked

https://www.weforum.org/agenda/2021/09/teams-
productivity-work-hours/

https://simplifyingmarketing.com/continuous-innovation/

https://elitebusinessmagazine.co.uk/analysis/item/pioneering-sustainability-a-blueprint-for-businesses-in-the-21st-century

https://www.linkedin.com/pulse/requirements-benefits-renewable-energy-systems-india-sumit-biswas

https://www.linkedin.com/pulse/how-build-effective-employee-reward-recognition-program-kiran-sira

https://aaronhall.com/insights/embracing-uncertainty-strategies-for-reinventing-your-career/

https://aaronhall.com/insights/unleashing-your-potential-the-path-to-success-and-fulfillment/

https://getbravo.io/employee-of-the-month-program/

https://yojanaonline.com/pm-vishwakarma-yojana/

https://www.sciencedirect.com/science/article/pii/S0264837719311779

https://www.academia.edu/115683128/Reservation_Policy_and_Social_Justice_in_India_A_Constitutional_Perspective

https://link.springer.com/chapter/10.1007/978-3-030-83209-4_6

https://jauntandjourney.com/traditional-arts-and-crafts-a-window-into-cultural-heritage/

https://www.hardwarezone.com.sg/tech-news-apple-estimated-have-spent-almost-100-billion-rd-over-past-5-years

https://www.linkedin.com/pulse/navigating-skills-gap-building-future-ready-workforce

https://timesofindia.indiatimes.com/blogs/voices/design-and-innovation-play-a-key-role-in-making-india-a-powerhouse-of-consumer-and-electronics-manufacturing/

https://rightasrain.uwmedicine.org/mind/well-being/take-risks-learn-from-failure

https://www.tandfonline.com/doi/full/10.1080/02601370.2023.2234133

https://delhipathshala.in/approaches-to-the-study-of-nationalism-in-india-nationalist-imperialist-marxist-and-subaltern/

https://en.wikipedia.org/wiki/Unnat_Jyoti_by_Affordable_LEDs_for_All

https://www.myscheme.gov.in/schemes/ddugku

https://enlightio.com/why-is-patriotism-important

https://ritusacademy.com/patriotism-meaning-types-and-importance/

https://pib.gov.in/PressReleaseIframePage.aspx?PRID=1882145

https://www.weforum.org/agenda/2021/09/teams-productivity-work-hours/

https://www.thehindu.com/business/Economy/understanding-worker-productivity-and-how-it-relates-to-economic-growth-explained/article67490775.ece
https://www.insightsonindia.com/2023/10/30/workers-productivity-long-working-hours/

https://ourworldindata.org/working-hours

https://ourworldindata.org/grapher/productivity-vs-annual-hours-worked

https://www.worldbank.org/en/research/employing-workers/data/working-hours

https://bhr-navigator.unglobalcompact.org/issues/working-time/

https://www.hibob.com/blog/hr-challenges-in-multinational-companies/

https://www.un.org/development/desa/dspd/wp-content/uploads/sites/22/2022/06/Verick_Labour-market-trends-longer-term-challenges-and-impact-of-crises.pdf

https://www.ilo.org/global/about-the-ilo/newsroom/news/WCMS_670171/lang--en/index.htm

https://www.enterprisetimes.co.uk/2018/10/16/how-can-technology-help-with-time-management/

https://www.eleapsoftware.com/glossary/strategies-for-managing-work-hours-effectively/

https://simpleprogrammer.com/time-management-apps/

https://www.evalflow.com/blog/the-role-of-technology-in-modern-performance-management

https://ecommons.cornell.edu/bitstream/handle/1813/75082/Collins4_The_Relationship_of_Achievement_Motivation_post_print.pdf?sequence=1

https://blog.hubspot.com/sales/achievement-motivation

https://www.timeetc.com/resources/how-to-achieve-more/why-motivation-matters-the-key-to-success-for-entrepreneurs

https://byjus.com/question-answer/describe-briefly-the-role-of-achievement-motivation-in-entrepreneurship/

https://nios.ac.in/media/documents/249_Enterpreneurship/English_pdf/249_Enterpreneurship_Lesson_8.pdf

https://www.msn.com/en-in/news/other/bengaluru-startups-twist-to-narayana-murthys-70-hour-work-week-advice-wins-the-internet-watch/ar-BB1lGGmW

https://www.msn.com/en-in/news/india/angry-rantmans-death-his-last-rant-was-against-nr-narayana-murthys-70-hour-work-week-what-he-said/ar-AA1nfvbU

Unleashing India's Potential: 70 Hr. Weekly Workhour

https://timesofindia.indiatimes.com/business/india-business/narayana-murthy-says-indian-youth-should-work-70-hours-a-week-not-pick-undesirable-habits-from-the-west/articleshow/104732137.cms

https://bing.com/search?q=Narayana+Murthy+advocate+longer+work+hours+for+India%27s+Youth ""

https://www.oneindia.com/india/should-indian-youth-work-70-hours-a-week-narayana-murthys-suggestion-ignites-debate-on-x-3668867.html ""

https://www.indiatoday.in/technology/news/story/infosys-founder-narayana-murthy-says-young-it-workers-should-work-70-hours-a-week-new-work-culture-is-needed-2454047-2023-10-26

*********************The End*********************